D1596978

Date: 5/24/22

658.15224 GIL
Gildin, Norman B.,
Learn from my experiences :
a

PALM BEACH COUNTY
LIBRARY SYSTEM
3650 SUMMIT BLVD.
WEST PALM BEACH, FL 33406

LEARN FROM MY EXPERIENCES

A Collection of **Essays** on **Fundraising** for Professionals, Lay Leaders, Volunteers and the Public

"MAY YOUR CHARITY INCREASE AS MUCH AS YOUR WEALTH" *Proverb*

NORMAN B. GILDIN

Learn from My Experiences: A Collection of Essays on Fundraising
for Professionals, Lay Leaders, Volunteers and the Public

First Edition 2021

Published by BookBaby 7905 N. Crescent Blvd. Pennsauken, NJ 08110
www.bookbaby.com

© 2021 Norman B. Gildin. All rights reserved.

Publisher's Cataloging-in-Publication data

Name: Gildin, Norman B., author
Title: Learn from my experiences: a collection of essays on fundraising for professionals,
lay leaders, volunteers and the public / Norman B. Gildin.
Description: Pennsauken, NJ: BookBaby, 2021.
Identifiers: LCCN: 2021921804 | ISBN: 978-1-66781-551-0 (hardcover)
| 978-1-66781-151-2 (Softcover) | 978-1-66781-152-9 (eBook)
Subjects: LCSH Fund raising. | Nonprofit organizations--Management.
| BISAC BUSINESS & ECONOMICS / Nonprofit Organizations
& Charities / Fundraising & Grants | BUSINESS & ECONOMICS
/ Nonprofit Organizations & Charities / Management & Leadership
Classification: LCC HD62.6 .G55 2021 | DDC 658.15/224--dc23

*No part of this publication may be reproduced, distributed, or transmitted in any form
or by any means, including photocopying, recording, or other electronic or mechanical
methods, without the prior written permission of the publisher, except in the case of brief
quotations embodied in critical reviews and certain other noncommercial uses permitted
by copyright law. For permission requests, contact BookBaby at* info@bookbaby.com *or
Norman B. Gildin at* ngildin@gmail.com, www.StrategicFundraisingGroup.com.

ISBN 978-1-66781-551-0 (Hardcover Edition)
ISBN 978-1-66781-151-2 (Softcover Edition)
ISBN 978-1-66781-152-9 (eBook)

Library of Congress Control Number - 2021921804

Photography Credit: Sivan Ravit

Printed and bound in the United States

Table of Contents

DEDICATIONS

Dedicated

In Loving Memory

Of my Dear Parents,

Cantor Ihil and Charlotte (Lazar) Gildin, OBM,

In Loving Memory

Of my Dear Brother,

Abe Gildin, OBM,

In Loving Memory

Of my Dear In-Laws,

Abe and Sari Baron, OBM,

In Loving Memory

Of my Uncles, Aunts and Cousins, OBM,

Who perished in the Shoah,

And

In Loving Memory of the

Six Million Martyrs

Who perished in the Holocaust.

May their Names and Memories be for a Blessing.

FOREWORD

Common Sense.

Yes, common sense is what should drive a development executive in his or her work. This isn't rocket science. Not by any means. Don't let them tell you otherwise (whoever "them" is; there is always a "them").

Of course, one needs the right education (I have an MA from the George Washington University, School of Government & Business Administration), but it isn't mandatory. A CFRE (Certified Fundraising Executive) certificate is helpful, but also not mandatory. And a few other fixings should help, such as personal integrity and a moral compass, ingenuity, a dash of style, cleverness, humor and even boldness, a personality that works well with interpersonal relationships, passion about the work you do, confidence, intrinsic competences such as good organizational skills, some mentoring helps (see chapter called "Mentoring for Success") and a fire in the belly (see chapter called "A Fire in the Belly").

Now that you are getting ready to be a development executive, or even a veteran fundraiser, why do you need this book *Learn from My Experiences*?

My intention is to draw from my nearly four-and-a-half decades of fundraising experiences and provide anecdotal occurrences on the basis of facts, and not just supposition, that can assist the incoming development associate (aka the "newbie") to the veteran or senior development executive in a variety of ways and situations.

This book is meant to be an easy read. Like I said above, this isn't rocket science (although there is a chapter on fundraising in the year 2075; see Table of Contents). You can pick it up and read through the book, or just glance at the chapter headings in the Table of Contents and read chapters that interest you. Simple.

This book is intended to help not only development professionals, but also lay leaders, volunteers and even the public, who are involved in fundraising. Is it an exhaustive description of every kind of fundraising? No, but it does address the major categories of giving, namely, annual campaigns, capital campaigns, planned giving and endowment fund giving. Some more, some less—you be the judge.

It took me more than three years to write this book, and the last year of writing took place during the outbreak of the COVID-19 pandemic. In this regard, I have a section that just deals with COVID-19 pandemic issues that may be useful, or not. But let's just hope that we never face such a situation again in our lifetimes. It also was written during the Trump and Biden administrations, and some of my thinking was influenced by relevant national events and policies. But this is *not* a political book, nor does it cover political fundraising or political contributions.

In 2012, I established a consulting company called Strategic Fundraising Group LLC. This also gave me pause to see things from the other side of the table. As a fundraising consultant, you get to see the sophistication as well as the lack of sophistication that some nonprofits possess. With 1.6 million registered nonprofits in the United States, there is a vast range in the understanding of fundraising.

I hope this book meets your expectations. If it doesn't, at least you should know that I tried (oh well). My fervent wish is for much success in raising essential funds for your organization.

All the best.

—Norman B. Gildin

P.S. By the way, no computers or keyboards were harmed in the making of this book.

STRATEGIC
FUNDRAISING
GROUP LLC

ACKNOWLEDGMENTS

A book like this doesn't happen in a vacuum. It took four-and-a-half decades of heavy lifting to reach this point. Along the way, there were some key figures who earned my love, admiration and respect, whom I take this opportunity to acknowledge.

In the introduction to *Learn from My Experiences*, you will read about the various influencers in my life—religious, familial, academic and career. No need to repeat them. Suffice it to say that I wouldn't be here unless I had the strong support and involvement of those individuals who molded me and influenced my career path. Some are mentioned directly in this book.

I would be remiss if I didn't acknowledge the staff I recruited and/ or worked with me in my position as a senior development executive. Listing individuals by name risks leaving someone out. Nevertheless, please know that I am forever grateful to my teams who worked side-by-side with me and deserve special recognition. My sincerest thanks to everyone.

I also want to acknowledge four individuals who have published my columns in their newspapers and whose association gave me further impetus to write this book. They are Moshe Kinderlehrer and Jill Kirsch, Co-Founder/Co-Publisher and Senior Editor, respectively, of *The Jewish Link of New Jersey*; Alan Goch, Editor, Sun-Sentinel's *South Florida Jewish Journal*; and Kari Barnett, Editor, Sun-Sentinel's *Gateway Gazette*. I am grateful to them for publishing the columns I send them regularly, many that made it into this book.

Finally, I also want to thank the one and only Nachum Segal, founder of JM in the AM and the Nachum Segal Network, and a major radio, online and Internet streaming personality, who has been at his craft for soon-to-be forty years. There were many instances when I appeared on his radio shows, and can directly attribute the success of events or activities I promoted to his involvement. He is a larger-than-life persona that has greatly impacted the greater Jewish community, and beyond.

Foremost in my thanks, however, is my family. They put up with me during the good times and the not-so-good times. They always encouraged me and gave me the inspiration to continue, persevere and succeed. Kudos.

I thank my children, Jonathan, Alex, Jennifer, Eli and Joshy, for hanging in there with me and for solemnly attending the dinners, concerts and golf tournaments, among other activities they obligingly graced with their presence or helped me bring about. Later, as each child married, their spouses took turns, as well, in being good sports. Thank you to Leah (Grunspan), Shirley (Lax), Joshua (Lowy), Leah (Moskowitz) and Chani (Colton) for taking part when called upon. And they all have blessed my wife and me with the greatest grandchildren. We couldn't be prouder.

Most of all, I acknowledge my loving wife, Barbara, who really put up with me through thick or thin and faithfully shared the good times and the bad. Barb, you are the love of my life, and I am eternally grateful to you for being my sounding board, my lifetime mate and companion, and for finding the silver lining in the clouds when it was necessary (and for putting away the shekels that made our retirement possible). Love you.

—Norman B. Gildin

P.S. And yes, thank you, Cookie and Zeesie!

INTRODUCTION

How did I become a fundraiser? The answer requires sharing some of my background and how I reached this point in my life. So, bear with me as I try to expound without boring you (too much).

Religious Influences

It all started when I was eight years old. My parents and I lived in Polanco, Mexico, where my father, Cantor Ihil Gildin, OBM, held a position as the cantor of Congregation Beis Yitzchak. The Shamash (Sexton) of the Shul (synagogue) was a kindly, older gentleman by the name of Reb Ben Zion (I do not remember his last name). It was customary during morning and evening services for the Shamash to make the rounds in the Shul with a charity box and for congregants to insert their daily contribution. It was also called the "Bedek Habayis" fund (Hebrew for the "House Maintenance" fund).

One day, Reb Ben Zion turned to me and asked me to take the tzedakah (charity) box around the synagogue. The congregants greeted me with a smile as I ventured from one person to the next. I liked the feeling, and soon it became my daily job to carry around the tzedakah box. It was my first exposure to fundraising. And I really cherished that feeling.

The next recollection I have of being exposed to fundraising was when we moved to Washington, DC, when I was eleven years old and I went with my father into the Shul office. I listened intently to a conversation between my father and the executive director about High Holiday ticket sales. The synagogue sold upwards of eighteen hundred tickets for the High Holidays. The synagogue's accordion doors in the back always were opened yearly to accommodate the overflow crowd that came to listen to my father chant the services with the highly acclaimed High Holiday choir. Those tickets were vital to the synagogue budget, and the annual sales were considered a large fundraiser for the congregation. The closer you sat to the front, the more expensive the tickets were. The idea of raising funds was imprinted in my young mind, and it stuck.

Finally, and most important of all, it is my strong belief in Judaism and genuine appreciation for the need of tzedakah (charity) that propelled me in this direction. In the eleventh and final weekly portion in the *Book of Exodus*, it was after the incident when Moses smashed the Tablets of the Covenant on the Golden Calf that he harnessed the fervor of the children of Israel towards a more productive project: the creation of the Tabernacle in the desert. This Tabernacle went with them throughout their travels to the promised land. What is pertinent, however, is that Moses asked the people to bring him contributions towards the construction of this house of God. At one point, Moses even had to ask them to stop making contributions when enough was collected. Also, what is fascinating about this saga is that ethical procedures were eventually developed for ensuring accountability and transparency in the use of public funds. But what resonated with me about this episode, over most, was the essential nature of fundraising— funds earmarked for a worthy goal.

Familial Influences

My father, Cantor Ihil Gildin, OBM, was born in Romania. He was a lyric tenor and a liturgical cantor at Beth Sholom Synagogue in Washington, DC, his last held position. He passed away when I was only fourteen years old. He left me and my widowed mother, Charlotte (Shari) Lazar Gildin, OBM, who had to fend for both of us. She was born in Hungary, albeit she always kept a public persona that she was born in Czechoslovakia. She felt an inherent fear of being deported even though she was a legally naturalized US citizen.

What is clear is that I learned my values, outlook on life and work ethics from both of my parents. They each transmitted to me the importance of integrity, decency and to always preserve a moral compass. I learned the significance of aspiring to perfection from my father; he was meticulous in his handwriting, a perfectionist in his musical renditions and fastidious about his work as a former watchmaker. I learned the meaning of kindness to others from my mother, a Holocaust survivor; she never raised her voice, and treated everyone with respect and dignity. In their own ways, my parents set the table for me in life, and I am forever grateful for their influence and love.

My two older half-brothers (Leib and Abe) were married and lived in New York. Unfortunately, we had minimal contact with them, and my mother eked out a nominal living once she resorted to supplying room and board in our apartment to out-of-town businessmen. She also resumed her work as a seamstress, her vocation prior to marriage. We lived on this income, plus her monthly Social Security. Unfortunately, my late father left behind little in his estate, and it wasn't easy for my mother to make ends meet. Both of my brothers took their portions of the estate as they had growing families. It didn't make me happy because of our circumstances, but they were rightfully entitled to their share.

Academic Influences

Writing wasn't always a passion of mine. In fact, growing up in Washington, DC, I was a mediocre student. My grades were average and nothing about which to write home. More about my writing later.

While I was an unexceptional student, I somehow managed to graduate from the Hebrew Academy of Washington and then from the Yeshiva High School of Greater Washington. My grades were pathetic, but adequate to get me through high school. Don't ask.

In high school, I was under the guidance of two wonderful and support-ive individuals who took me under their wing for which I will always be grateful. Mrs. Hedy Peyser, who was the administrator/principal at the Yeshiva High School of Greater Washington, and Mrs. Tzivia Bramson, who also was the principal of general studies, were instru-mental in giving me initial direction in life. They patiently worked with me, and their confidence encouraged me in a positive way to care more about my studies. I must say, however, that when they arranged for me to take an aptitude test, I wasn't certain what to make of it. It showed that my career trajectory was to become an undertaker. Fortunately, that turned out to be a dead issue.

One more moderating influence on me was Rabbi Zechariah Mines, OBM, one of my rabbis at Yeshiva High School. Rabbi Mines was a mild-mannered man with a pristine moral and ethical compass. He drew important distinctions between right and wrong that uncultivated high school students like me desperately needed to discern. These values guided me well in my work ethic and, in general, through-out life.

I eventually applied to Yeshiva University and was accepted on proba-tion to Yeshiva College. If I didn't do well, it would be my first and only semester there. Somehow, I managed to get through with average grades that first year, but at least I got through.

What turned me around was meeting the love of my life who gifted me with five wonderful children. I met Barbara (Baron) at Pioneer Country Club in upstate New York in the Catskill Mountains where I worked in 1971 as a summer busboy (eventually worked up as the captain of waiters). She was there for an NCSY convention. It became clear to me that, if I was going to get serious with my future life companion, then I had better get my act together. I decided to major in speech and drama, and in the end graduated Yeshiva University with honors—*magna cum laude*. But I still needed direction in life, because an untalented, starving actor or public speaker weren't ways to make a living.

There were two great influences on me at Yeshiva University. The first positive influencer was Dr. Arthur Tauber, the physical education and fencing coach, a legendary former Olympian and war hero. Professor Tauber gave me the career direction I urgently needed. Ironically, we only met on a few occasions, but these sessions were very productive. In our first encounter, he showed me the organization chart of a hospital in which he was the assistant administrator. It stimulated my interest in health-care administration, which helped launch my first career. Subsequently, he involved me in tutoring children from impoverished families, and I ended up spending several semesters at the George Washington High School in Washington Heights, New York, tutoring disadvantaged children with their reading skills. *It taught me a valuable lesson in giving back to the community.*

The second major influencer was someone I had been warned could be the end of me at Yeshiva College. Friends who took his speech course cautioned me that he destroyed the career path of many students. I was warned to stay away from him, if possible. When I registered in my freshman year, as the luck of the draw would have it, I ended up in his speech course. Pleading with the registrar to move me to another speech class was futile, and frightening. The instructor's name was the late Anthony Beukas (later Dr. Anthony Beukas). I was resigned to the fact that my stay at Yeshiva College would be short-lived, and I resolved to just make the best of it.

The first assignment in his speech class was to create a speech using a precisely organized outline. The idea was to properly structure your thoughts on paper before delivering the speech so that you don't ramble. But it had to follow a certain format, which wasn't entirely clear to me. Uh oh.

The day the outlines were due came and went. I had "worked my kishkes out" (Jewish expression that loses in the translation, but you should get the idea) getting this outline ready—that, and a hope and a prayer.

Dr. B (as we later called him) returned the graded outlines the following week. I sat near the front of the classroom and could see the grades as he was sorting them out: a lot of Cs and Ds, and some Fs. My heart sank. He distributed them to the class, and many a groan was heard. Finally, all the papers were returned; all but one—mine. I was getting increasingly nervous.

Dr. B then launched into what sounded like what was going to be a tirade. His voice kept on getting louder and louder. He began like this. "There is one paper I am not returning. I simply can't." He coughed and cleared his throat a few times. "This outline doesn't deserve to be with the others." Oh no! "I simply don't know how to describe it to you." Oy vey! And then, looking around the room, he said this in his loudest voice: "It was the finest speech outline I have ever received in all the freshman classes I have taught over the years." With that, he turned to me and announced, "Mr. Gildin, your outline was exceptional, A+, and I am keeping it to share with future classes." You could have bowled me over with the proverbial feather.

This was a turning point in my college career, and it set me on a path to success. Thank you, Dr. Beukas! This wasn't fundraising, but it was a critical motivating moment. It showed me what I needed to do to excel in whatever career I chose. (Teacher's pet notwithstanding, to be truthful, I think he really lost the paper.)

Career Influences

During my career, I primarily had three mentors (whom I discuss in the chapter entitled "Mentoring for Success"):

1) Dennis J. Magid—Jewish Home for the Elderly of Fairfield County, Fairfield, Connecticut
2) Eli S. Feldman—Metropolitan Jewish Geriatric Foundation, Brooklyn, New York
3) David Mandel—OHEL Children's Home and Family Services, Brooklyn, New York

But I want to acknowledge them here for their constant encouragement, understanding the importance of fundraising and their different styles of fundraising administration, which were significant influences on my career during which I raised upwards of $93 million. You can follow my career path in their organizations by checking my LinkedIn page under @Ngildin.

However, there is one more individual I must recognize, especially since his influence over me was on my writing ability and honing my public relations and marketing skills. In the chapter titled "Is Fundraising a Solo Act," I reference Howard J. Rubenstein, the late public relations guru, whom I worked with for ten years when Metropolitan Jewish Health System became one of his accounts. While I learned much from Howard, it was the senior account executive he assigned to me from whom I developed my skills and passion for writing. His name was Sy Schwartz.

Sy's office was down the hall from Howard's, which tells you the value that Rubenstein placed in him. Sy reminded me of the intrepid reporter with a grey fedora slightly tilted forward on his head, a #2 pencil perched over one ear and a half-lit cigarette drooping from the right side of his mouth. He actually typed his copy on an old Smith Corona typewriter.

Sy was a super-confident executive who felt every story he wrote was important and would be picked up by the news media. He was an exceptional writer, and I attribute much of my writing skills and passion to Sy. He also knew how to pitch a story to the media and get it published. Sy understood the value of a press release, a public service announcement (PSA) and the critical nature of marketing a program so that it would generate interest among the masses.

Sy's understanding of PR helped us achieve financial success at the Metropolitan Jewish Geriatric Foundation with our $16 million capital campaign for the to-be-constructed Shorefront Jewish Geriatric Center. He was instrumental in editing and developing copy for our capital campaign, case statement, newsletters, ancillary brochures, script materials for our video releases and so much more. I tip my hat to Sy for his profound influence on me. He was the one who ignited my excitement for writing. His untimely passing left a void in my life.

Conclusion

A favorite saying of mine is found in Psalm 199:99 and derived from *Ethics of the Fathers* 4:1: *"Mikol melamdai hiskalti,"* which means "From all my teachers I grew wise." This signifies that, what I attained in life and in the world of fundraising, I gained from the wise people around me—the influencers in my sphere. I thank them sincerely for sharing their knowledge to make me a better man, a better fundraiser.

CHAPTER ONE
Why Do People Give?

What motivates you to get up in the morning? Your job? Family responsibilities? A game of golf or tennis? Everyone has something that motivates them to do what they do. This holds true just as well for philanthropy. People are motivated to give for a reason. They may not admit to it, but they are.

Usually when a donor connects with the mission of a nonprofit, that's all it takes to motivate him/her to give. You'll hear someone say that it's their "pet project," and this is because they feel close to the organization or identify with its services, staff or clients. Perhaps there is a history that connected them or their family.

In the *Mishnah Torah*, under laws of charity, the author Maimonides identified eight levels of charity. Each step is higher than the next. The highest level, above which there is no greater, is to support a fellow Jew by endowing him with a gift or loan, or entering into a partnership with him or finding employment for him, in order to strengthen his hand so that he will not need to be dependent upon others . . . Perhaps, Maimonides affirmed these levels because everyone has a different ability to give. I assert everyone has a different reason why they give.

So, what motivates a person to give in one level versus another? Everyone is different, and yet charity is a commonality we all share, but for different reasons.

Studies have been done to learn why people give. For the fundraiser, understanding this can mean the difference between success and failure. If you figure out what motivates a donor to give, half the battle is won. This is important not just because it helps the fundraiser in his or her quest, but it hopefully helps achieve the philanthropic needs of the donor.

So why do people give? Let me suggest there are many reasons. The following represent only some:

1) Here's a surprise. Half of the people give to a charity for one reason and one reason alone—they were asked. So, this teachable moment is a simple lesson. You have a 50 percent chance for success simply by asking. The donor may or may not have a special motivation.

2) Some folks have an inherent religious belief learned when they were young. There are those who believe in tithing: giving a tenth of their earnings, also called "Ma'aser," (Hebrew) to charity. Others give to mark a yahrzeit (anniversary of the death of a loved one) or for Yizkor (Hebrew prayer recited on designated Jewish holidays), prior to a Jewish holiday, to commemorate a happy occasion or sometimes a sad one.

3) This may surprise you, too. Some persons contribute as a means to self-preservation. How, you may ask? For the answer, go no further than reading the mantras of several nonprofits. For instance, the American Cancer Society states: "We want to wipe out cancer in your lifetime." When AIDS was at its peak, the mantra was, "Unless a cure is found for this killer disease, millions of people may die." Some people feel that by giving to a certain cause, they may avoid the nasty tentacles of the disease.

4) No surprise with this reason—guilt. This occurs when people feel they will neglect or have neglected the needs of others. Commercials that portray neglected animals, the homeless or wounded veterans are prime examples of hammering home guilt.

5) Tax benefits are a sure-shot method of inducing donations. Deductions are not what they used to be, and who knows what laws Congress may add, yet tax advantages are still a big seller. This is especially true with planned gifts such as charitable trusts and gift annuities.

6) College graduates often become indebted to their alma mater, families benefit by the admission of a loved one into a nursing home and congregants benefit from membership in a synagogue. What these have in common is a *moral* obligation to support the institution that has done good in their eyes.

7) Donor recognition is a motivator for some. It can come in the form of an award presented at an event, a plaque on a wall, an honor roll or even a listing in an annual report or newsletter. To some degree, this also plays to the ego of the philanthropist.

8) Peer pressure works well as a motivator for some folks. During a solicitation, it often helps to have present a family member, a friend or a business associate whom the donor respects. That kind of leverage can go a long way.

9) Here's probably the most important reason of all: *making a difference.* Many individuals want to know that they are making a difference in the lives of those less fortunate. Philanthropists such as Bill and Melinda Gates, who give billions away to the African continent for vaccines, AIDS support and the like, genuinely feel they are making a difference in millions of lives. And they do.

There may be other reasons why people give to charitable causes, but these are at the top of my list. So, when you see others giving to their favorite nonprofit, you will have insight into their reasoning.

So, I ask you: why do *you* give?

CHAPTER TWO
Is This the Time
to Start Up a Nonprofit?

I am periodically approached by individuals who wish to start up a nonprofit organization. During the COVID-19 pandemic, my skepticism abounded whether it was the right time or the right environment. Across the country, stories teemed with how synagogues, Jewish community centers, Jewish social service agencies and many Jewish nonprofit institutions were struggling to make ends meet. They were either closing their doors or furloughing staff because they could not afford the overhead. It was a sad state of affairs.

But, if the past is any prologue to the future, we are rebounding and, once we do, life will resume, and normalcy will return. *Yesh Tikvah* (Hebrew for "there is reason to hope"). While the COVID-19 era was a questionable time to start up a nonprofit, planning began for some. Here are the *essential* and hard questions to ask that will dictate whether to start a new cause.

Defined Need

Some begin this quest because they think it's a good idea. My first question is this: did you define the need? Was there a problem in your community that is unresolved, and does your program fill the gap in the area lacking services? Do you have statistics or metrics to back up your idea showing a definite need?

Alternative or Similar Services

Have you investigated whether your idea is truly unique? Are there similar or overlapping services already in place? What other options are available in the community that target the population you want to serve, and are they adequately meeting the needs?

Service Area

Thought must be given to serving a geographic area that makes sense and doesn't stretch your resources to the limits. Do you know where your home base will be, and is this a service that can be supported financially in a limited locale, or is it worthy of serving a region, state or nationally?

Constituency Base

Are there others who share your excitement and interest? Will they be willing to help this undertaking with their volunteer time, leadership and/or other resources? Have you explored whether there exists a constituency that is willing and able to support the cause personally and financially?

Mission Statement

What is the purpose of your organization? Have you established a mission statement that describes your raison d'etre, your reason for being? Is there a proclamation or guiding statement that declares your commitment, and how do you plan to pursue it?

Registrations

There are various registrations that are needed to give your nonprofit its formal status, and essential to this is securing federal tax exempt status. Achieving 501 (c) (3) standing is necessary so that donors can claim tax deductions for their charitable gifts. In addition, there may be state registrations, as well as rankings you need to meet as defined by independent charity watchdogs such as Charity Navigator or GuideStar.

Governing Body

Part of being a responsible nonprofit is setting up a group of volunteers that will set policy, govern, advocate on your behalf and help philanthropically. The board of directors should set up a budget, conduct oversight, institute accountability, evaluate progress and, if justified, recruit a senior executive to run the organization.

Create a Database

Do you know your supporters? What are their demographics? Are they capable of consistently helping the organization? Will some offer to volunteer and others have the capacity to make small or large charitable gifts? Will they be willing to bring others into the fold? Can this important information be put into a workable database?

Informational Meetings

Are you prepared to set up receptions, or informational get-togethers, with community members and lay leaders to tell your story? Reaching the masses is an important way to get your message across and is important to mobilizing grassroots support. Are you ready to galvanize public enthusiasm on your behalf?

Marketing and Fundraising

Have you given thought to developing a marketing plan that delineates how you will publicize your services through press releases, advertising, promotions, speaking engagements, print and electronic media and the like? Your marketing plan should complement a strategic fundraising plan that will help you raise the necessary funds to support your nonprofit.

No one said this would be easy. Not every nonprofit has gone through these steps, but the successful ones have. Think about it, and then ask yourself: "Is this the time to start up my nonprofit?"

23

CHAPTER THREE
The Great Divide:
Millennials vs. Baby Boomers

Fundraising has a long and storied history going back at least to the time when the Jews traveled in the desert and Moses collected funds to pay for the building and the upkeep of the Mishkan (Tabernacle). Every Israelite over the age of twenty was commanded to donate one half Shekel to the Mishkan project. That capital campaign was a huge success!

Of course, there was no other nonprofit organization competing for scarce funds, as there are today.

Fast forward to the present day.

According to a story in *Giving USA*, "Donations from America's individuals, estates, foundations and corporations reached an estimated $373.25 billion in 2015, setting a record for the second year in a row." Individual donors led the way with a whopping $264.58 billion, 3.8 percent more than the year before, and followed a pattern seen over more than six decades. *Giving USA 2020* in an update shared even more impressive figures: "American individuals, bequests, foundations and corporations gave an estimated $449.64 billion to U.S. charities in 2019, placing it among the highest years ever for charitable giving." We already know that preliminary indications show even bigger gains during the COVID-19 pandemic.

The National Center for Charitable Statistics also states that there are roughly 1.6 million registered nonprofit organizations in the United States today. This is nearly a 27 percent increase in nonprofits since 2000 alone. But there also are 2.3 million nonprofits in the United States. However, not all are registered as tax-exempt organizations.

In the more than four decades I worked in the field of development (the professional name for the field of fundraising), I have seen seismic changes in philanthropy as generational transformations occurred and are happening even now. This is what I call "The Great Divide: Millennials versus Baby Boomers." This gulf is typified with characteristics now evolving as a new face of philanthropy takes shape.

The Baby Boomers

Baby Boomers were born between 1946 and 1964, give or take a year. There are now more than 77 million Baby Boomers, according to a 2017 story in *The Motley Fool.* Early on, I found that this generation of donors had certain distinctive qualities. They loved special events. Dinners, concerts, raffles, journals were only among some of the methods of fundraising they regularly subscribed to. This group also enjoyed attending board and committee meetings. It was traditional.

I remember collating dozens of dinner and journal information kits that we distributed to committees with suggestions and tips on how to go about engaging their families, friends and acquaintances to participate in the gala. One day, an irate committee member called me and demanded to know: "Where is my checklist of those I need to solicit?" She was referring to a prospect list including her accountant, attorney, refuse collector, landscaper and others which was inadvertently left out of her kit. Most of the list was common sense, but she was lost without it.

This generation had a unique work ethic that manifested itself in fundraising. We used to run a mid-summer raffle and gala event at one of my nonprofits. Irving, a polish Holocaust survivor, was our most prolific raffle fundraiser, bringing in twenty-five to thirty thousand dollars in raffle sales each year.

Here is how Irving worked. We would be sitting in the board room at a non-fundraising meeting with twenty or more in attendance. Irving would drop by unannounced and poke his head into the conference room and innocently ask in his strong Yiddish accent: "Am I disturbing you?" And for the next thirty minutes, Irving would regale us with his raffle stories. We loved it and knew there was no sense in continuing our meeting. Irving's work ethic was unassailable.

Social media was not in place then, and Baby Boomers relied on phone squads, letters and personal contacts to reach those donors. Obviously, times have changed, and today we strongly rely on technology to get the word out. Yet, managing personal relationships has not changed and is as important today as it was then.

Don't doubt for a moment that the Baby Boomers haven't adapted today; they also use social media and other online methods to give. But there was a different relationship one had with the Baby Boomers, and they responded to different giving catalysts.

The Millennials

The face of fundraising has changed dramatically, and Millennials, born after 1981, best exemplify a new approach. I met with a young financial investor in Los Angeles a few years ago to solicit a gift. His immediate response was, "Show me your metrics." He had no interest in my emotional stories about the organization. He wanted to see our budget and the measurement data showing the nonprofits' progress.

According to a 2019 Pew Research Center study, there were an estimated 72.1 million Millennials in the United States, and they are very tech savvy and more involved in business. The donor of yesteryear was happy to write a check and get an ad in a journal or a plaque on a wall. Today's donor is no longer satisfied with these amenities. Instead, among their interests, they want to see the nonprofits' website, their Charity Navigator rating, mobile device giving, strong social networking outreach, monthly giving options, crowdsourcing, GoFundMe page and special events that cater to large singles or young couples' activities.

Millennials, more than before, seldom have the attention span of their elders. Today's Facebook and Twitter media may lose their interest as new and more interesting social media are developed. If you don't respond immediately to their needs, they will likely go elsewhere. Their passion for the charity must mix with fun and social networking. We need to adapt.

Reaching New Fundraising Plateaus

I am convinced that there is no word in the Hebrew language that is not also the name of a Jewish nonprofit. If someone sneezes and a friend says, "Labriut" (Hebrew for "to your good health"), inevitably someone else will claim it and say, "Great name for an organization." The intense competition for the same fundraising dollars will require creative new ideas to reach Baby Boomers, Millennials and others. This will necessitate reaching new fundraising plateaus.

Is your organization up to the Millennial challenge?

CHAPTER FOUR
The Art of Storytelling

There's an old saying: "Those who tell the stories rule the world." One thing for sure—if you are a fundraiser and you can tell a good story, it is likely that you will thrive.

There are generally three types of philanthropists. The first type wants to hear heartrending stories about how their uplifting contributions improve the plight of those less fortunate. The second type is not interested in listening to stories that melt the heart. Give them metrics. Give them financial statements, numbers and budget figures. That's it. The third type falls in between, and looks for a little of each approach.

Let's focus on the storyteller who supplies meaningful joy to a donor seeking his compassion quotient.

Working at a nonprofit Jewish home for the elderly had many benefits for me. The environment was warm, the care compassionate and the quality of life for the residents outstanding. A plethora of stimulating programs to enhance the dignity and self-esteem of the older residents was of utmost importance. All of these made for wonderful stories we could share with contributors.

In the facility, I opened a sheltered workshop (work activity center) where residents were paid for their work productivity. Projects ranged from assembling children's game pieces into boxes to sorting employee timecards to collecting bath sets in a pretty satchel tethered to a colorful cellophane-covered basket.

One morning on my way to the office, I passed a ninety-four-year-old resident making his way to the workshop. He was in a rush, and I stopped him for a fleeting moment and asked, "Harry, where are you running?" Without missing a step, Harry turned to me as he wended his way down the hall and said, "Can't talk now. On my way to work and I am late!" Can you imagine, a nonagenarian whose life focus was work productivity? What a great story to share with donors deeply touched by our ability to supply consequential life and job opportunities to the aged residents. And they got paid! It enhanced the fundraising campaign that year.

Another Jewish nonprofit I worked for provided residential services to developmentally disabled adults who, otherwise, could not care for themselves. When I started working there, I went through an intensive orientation to learn about its essential services to the community. One day I visited a small group residence and was in for a remarkable surprise.

First, let's take a trip in my time machine. In 1969, an ambitious young journalist by the name of Geraldo Rivera aired an investigative exposé about a mental institution called Willowbrook where patients lived in the most deplorable and neglected living conditions. It was shocking and appalling that such an institution existed in the United States. Geraldo revealed many abuses and uncovered the horrific conditions these patients lived in. His muckraking was the catalyst to improving the lives of the mentally disabled.

Let's return now to my visit at the adult group residence. I walked into the home and met clients who were previously institutionalized in Willowbrook. What an amazing encounter. The residents were dressed in neat, clean and comfortable clothing, and lived in a warm and homelike atmosphere. The pleasing scent of a homemade meal was in the air and I wanted to stay for dinner. It smelled so good. The residence was pristine clean and everyone—clients, staff and volunteers—greeted me with a smile. What a great story to relate to our donors. Our supporters were awestruck and spellbound.

The most important task of a fundraiser is to inspire folks who contribute to our causes. We must empower donors to aid us in our quest to improve the human condition. When we share heartwarming stories about those in our charge and how we provide them with a sense of purpose and a better life, it elevates our mission in the eyes of our benefactors. And if they connect with our mission and trust us, we accomplish our goal and raise crucial funds for the organization.

As a child, I loved stories my mother read to me. My children loved stories I read them. And now my grandchildren love the stories I read them. Many of our donors love to hear success stories if they are true and poignant.

Have you heard about the "two-minute elevator speech"? It's the limited time we occasionally need to empower a patron with the empathy required to make a generous gift. That's the epitome of good storytelling.

Are you up to the challenge? In that case, have I got a story for you!

STRATEGIC
FUNDRAISING
GROUP LLC

CHAPTER FIVE
A Path to Empathy

Marlon Brando is among a group of actors best known for a technique called "Method Acting." It is a type of acting that interprets sincere and emotionally expressive performances by fully inhabiting the role of the character. It is an actor's path to empathy.

Others who have used this technique include Konstantin Stanislavski, Lee Strassberg, Bradley Cooper, Robert DeNiro, Heath Ledger, Sylvester Stallone among many famous, and not-so-famous, actors. Some thespians become so immersed in their role that they don't break out of character until the part is over. While some consider this method extreme, nevertheless, it helps the actor achieve a genuine consciousness of the character.

It is said that the power of empathy is seeing the world through another's eyes. The late Rabbi Lord Jonathan Sacks said, "The *Torah* is essentially a book of law. Why then contain narrative at all? Because law without empathy equals justice without compassion." We learn that Judaism encourages a path to empathy even as a way to treat the stranger in our land.

Sadly, there were times during my career when I felt that some fund-raising professionals lacked an intrinsic empathy for those they served (and this is purely my subjective opinion). It should come as no surprise to anyone that some folks find themselves in positions that are not always suited to their temperament or personality. Everyone is built differently, and, sometimes, it is necessary for professionals to structurally develop an empathy for those they serve because they weren't born with such feelings or emotions.

Let me illustrate.

As a licensed nursing home administrator, it periodically came to my attention that staff were bothered by the complaints or whining of patients and/or their families. Sounds terrible, and it is. But the reality is that staff often tolerated complaints all day or all night long. It's not an easy job. Some suggest they get paid to endure complaints, but after a while staff become desensitized unless we instill a sense of empathy in them.

So, we created empathy classes for nurses, aides and other staff, designed to inculcate an improved understanding of the arduous circumstances in which patients and/or their families find themselves.

To enhance empathy, we sat staff in wheelchairs and asked them to move around the room only using their hands. Then we smeared Vaseline on makeshift eyeglasses for them to see what patients with vision problems experienced. Then we bound them in their wheelchairs to feel what it was like to be a patient in restraints. These exercises were invaluable in instilling and strengthening a sense of compassion for those we served. They were important pathways to empathy.

One Israel-based organization served impoverished children where families did not know whether they would even have food on the table for their next meal. The organization set up a wedding salon to provide needy brides with wedding dresses, shoes and other wedding accessories. They also set up day-care centers for indigent single mothers who spent days looking for gainful employment. Visiting these sites helped fundraising professionals develop a more sensitive perspective—empathy—for the plight these individuals faced.

In a program serving terminally ill patients, weekly patient-care conferences were held where an interdisciplinary team regularly met to discuss the needs of patients and their families. These sessions were indispensable to engendering empathy in attendees, as well as setting realistic life goals and care plans for patients.

I sat in on many conferences and listened to descriptions of serious medical diagnoses and patient setbacks. One could not help but feel a sense of profound empathy for patients, families and their ill-fated situations. While respecting privacy, fundraising professionals can be more effective in their role by communicating to philanthropists the sad state in which these individuals find themselves and, with the right support, how they can sustain themselves.

Empathy is a necessary attribute in any professional's understanding of the people he or she serves. Human beings are not widgets assembled on a conveyor belt. They live and breathe like you and me, and many do so under the most difficult conditions. Unless fundraisers place themselves in the shoes of those for whom they raise money, it will be tougher to raise vital funds to support their cause.

Everyone chooses their own path to empathy. Do you know yours?

CHAPTER SIX
Always Remember
to Say Thank You

My mother used to tell me when I received a gift or if someone did something nice for me, "Always remember to say thank you." Didn't your mother or parents do the same? When you are a little child, and growing up, this response just becomes a natural one and it is something you do by rote. It's automatic, or it should be. Little did I know then just how important such an innocuous message would become later in life.

Rabbi Berel Wein, a well-known rabbi, speaker and author, once wrote, "One of the cardinal principles of Judaism is gratitude—the necessity and ability to say thank you." In fact, he continues, "Jews begin their day with two words—*Modeh Ani*—I acknowledge and thank you God for having given me the gift of life once more as I awake to the new day." This is, perhaps, the ultimate thanks we can give.

Rabbi Wein admonishes those who don't follow this integral path in the Jewish heritage. He unequivocally states, "I am aware of fundraisers who feel no gratitude towards donors who somehow contribute less than the amount asked for or expected." Rabbi Wein concludes he "would say thank you to every donor with the same fervor and sincerity." And so should we.

Over the years, I learned that whether or not the donor contributed, or whether the level of gift was proportionate with ability, you always say thank you. It must be genuine, from the heart and sincere. One never takes for granted a kindness done by another person. Otherwise, also expect the donor to lower the bar next time or even decline to meet or consider a gift. Worse yet, I, as a Jew, would run the risk of committing a "chilul Hashem"—desecrating God's name and disgracing the organization I represented or even fellow Jews.

So, how does one say thank you to donors, or even prospects for giving? Of course, there are the conventional ways of doing so, including a heartfelt verbal expression of thanks, a written letter or a phone call. Today, things have changed and, depending on the level of gift, folks might get a text, an email or some other thanks via modern technology such as on WhatsApp. I foresee holographic projections in the future. Not so farfetched.

All of this presumes that we wait to thank a donor retroactively. What about being proactive and reaching out to donors or prospects prospectively? What? Thanking contributors before they give? That's right. We live in a highly competitive fundraising environment, and the nonprofit organization that thinks forward and creatively will be more successful than the one that is complacent and believes these things take care of themselves. They don't.

One important method of saying thanks is the daily Five to Ten Contact Points. I tried to call five to ten folks on my donor list every day to see how they were doing, give them a short progress report on my nonprofit or just acknowledge their past support. Imagine the donor's surprise that I did not call them to ask for a gift, but just to say thank you. The donor appreciates that I don't just eye them as "Mr. or Mrs. Moneybags," but acknowledge their priceless friendship.

Another proactive way to thank donors is to recognize their name, or insert a picture in your newsletter, annual report or other house organ for something other than a gift. Sometimes, this requires a donor's permission. They may want to remain anonymous. But that's okay. It's the thought that counts, and they will appreciate that you consulted them and wanted to acknowledge their generosity.

Clearly, there are more traditional methods of recognizing your donors. A commemorative plaque on a wall, asking them to be an honoree without strings attached at a special event, naming a program after the philanthropist are just some of the ways to say thank you. How many ways can you say thank you? Unlimited.

My mother, and probably your parents, were prescient when they inculcated in us the need to thank generosity and kindness in turn. As Rabbi Wein indicated, "The attitude of gratitude must always be present and must always find expression in actual deeds." This holds true for donors and for each other.

So, I ask, whom have you thanked today?

STRATEGIC
FUNDRAISING
GROUP LLC

CHAPTER SEVEN
A Thankless Job

It is often said that the Gabbai (Sexton) in the Shul has the most thankless job. He can never win. If he doesn't give someone an aliya (call up a congregant to the Torah reading), or doesn't call upon someone to lead services, or doesn't remember a yahrzeit (anniversary date of the death of a loved one), it's because he wasn't doing his job. He rarely gets thanked for the grief he endures and yet, amazingly, most Shuls have gabbaim with masochistic tendencies who, despite the agony, still volunteer and conscientiously do their job every day.

Mike Rowe is a TV commentator and author who hosts shows on Facebook. During one such show, he blasted politicians who deemed certain workers as essential and others as non-essential. This issue came up during a debate about lockdowns and whether certain businesses should be allowed to remain open or stay closed during the surge in COVID-19 cases. Much discussion proliferated over the airwaves and social media as to what workers should be considered *essential.* Rowe estimated that politicians declared 40 million Americans as *non-essential.* Talk about people having a thankless job!

I raise this issue because many development professionals have long felt that their job is a thankless one. Many feel taken for granted, while others are bothered by a lack of appreciation from their employer or board members. Welcome to the real world. The same can be said for many in other industries, such as the so-called *non-essential* worker. Or, how about one's spouse? Uh oh.

Do you feel taken for granted in your job? Do you feel underappreciated? Yes, this case can be made for many folks, so development professionals shouldn't feel unique membership to this club.

In February of 2020, I was elected as president of my Homeowners Association in Florida. It will take too long to explain how I found myself in that position (perhaps some other time). But talk about a thankless job! It is a volunteer position, but you wouldn't know it from the work it entails. It is a full-time job and is the equivalent of being the CEO of a nonprofit organization. In fact, our bylaws equated the president to a CEO. Nonetheless, it is a thankless job. But enough about me.

Having been in the development industry for decades, I understand why development professionals feel this way. It's quite simple. The development professional's philosophy should be to avoid narcissism nor claim credit for his or her success. Instead, they ought to regularly ascribe recognition to lay leaders who might not have put in even a fraction of the time or work required to achieve success. But the volunteer's title of chairman or co-chairman still adorns the fundraising invitation. That's like writing a story for a newspaper or magazine, but conferring the byline to the editor.

Development professionals often are immersed in a myriad of activities depending, of course, on the size, budget and needs of their nonprofit. For instance, when planning an event, they might secure sponsors, organize the committee, choose the event site, prepare and mail invitations, hire the caterer, coordinate the entertainment and the list goes on. That's often the professional's job. Yes, all of this, and then some, is often taken for granted by lay leaders, and sometimes even the professional's supervisor lacks appreciation. But that's the job, and it is frequently a thankless one.

One of my mentors once told me that part of my salary was getting paid for pain and anguish. I always took his opinion in stride. We also were taught that accolades were simply for lay leaders regardless of how much they involved themselves in the project. Remember this, development professional. If you want to motivate, *sincerely* motivate, lay leadership to be an integral member of your team, then be generous with *your* appreciation and compliments. To put it bluntly, that's how it works.

So, if you are in it because of the glory, or because you want everyone to know that the nonprofit's fundraising success is due to your shining brilliance, then you are in the wrong business. Spread the wealth, and the wealth of success will reflect on you. Otherwise, you may not be as indispensable as you think.

There is a saying: "That's the problem with putting others first; you've taught them you come second." As one media celebrity likes to say, "Now, thank me!"

STRATEGIC
FUNDRAISING
GROUP LLC

CHAPTER EIGHT
Are You a Leader or a Follower?

What is leadership, and who is a leader? There are countless tomes written on the subject enough to carry you to the Moon and back, if not farther. An article that once appeared in *Forbes* magazine defined leadership as "a process of social influence which maximizes the efforts of others, towards the achievement of a goal." My focus here is on leadership whose accomplishments improve society, not on evil despots.

Contrary to popular belief, leadership, the *Forbes* article continues, has nothing to do with a person's position in a company or organization. Just because you have seniority or are a chief executive officer doesn't make you a leader. Ever hear of the Peter Principle?

Individuals with charisma or those with a take-charge attitude don't automatically make leaders either, albeit we have suffered through enough cult leaders. Likewise, managers also are not necessarily leaders. One can manage things, but not necessarily people.

So, is a leader someone with followers? Not always. You can command a group of soldiers, but they *have* to follow orders. That does not always make the commander a leader. Some military leaders make dreadful mistakes.

What about a visionary who turns visions into reality? Is that person a leader? Not always, because a visionary doesn't constantly have a following that adheres to the vision. Albert Einstein was a genius, but not necessarily a leader.

Is someone who empowers others a leader? Empowering others is a noble virtue, but there are leaders who empower others to do bad things or follow a wrong course of action. So, that person isn't of necessity a leader either.

So, who is a fundraising leader?

My take is this: *the fundraising professional who consistently influences supporters in a positive way to achieve and secure their patronage and raises essential funds for the nonprofit is a fundraising leader.*

If we go back in history, we can fathom who were some of the great leaders. They include, among myriads others, Moses, Abraham Lincoln, Mahatma Gandhi, Golda Meir, Dr. Martin Luther King, Jr., and trailblazers such as Douglas MacArthur. These people embodied the essence of leadership.

President Ronald Reagan once said, "The greatest leader is not necessarily the one who does the greatest things. He is the one that gets the people to do the greatest things." Influencing philanthropically minded people to help others in a positive way is the mark of a true leader.

But what are the common traits that make up the DNA of an effective leader? Most experts tend to agree that it is a good communicator who inspires and unites others for a good cause. Usually, it is someone who leads by example. It is someone who takes responsibility and doesn't blame others for their shortcomings. Leaders are trustworthy and paradigms of integrity.

Speaker and author Michael G. Rogers tells a great story about leadership. Nearly 250 years ago, a man dressed in civilian clothes riding a horse came across a group of tired and weary soldiers who were digging a defensive position getting ready for the next battle. The leader of the beleaguered group was mean spirited and threatened to punish the soldiers for not digging fast enough. All he did was bark orders, but did not lift a finger to help.

The stranger on horseback queried the man in charge, "Why aren't you helping them?" The man snapped that he was in charge and they will "do as I tell them." He shouted at the stranger: "Help them yourself if you feel so strongly about it!"

To the surprise of the callous fellow, the stranger disembarked from the horse and helped the fatigued soldiers until the job was completed. He then congratulated the men for a job well done. He turned to the muddled leader of the crew and said, "You should notify top command next time your rank prevents you from supporting your men—and I will provide a more permanent solution."

It was then that the pompous autocrat learned a lesson in humility when he recognized the stranger as General George Washington.

Nonprofit professionals and fundraisers know that their job often requires them to roll up their sleeves and get down and dirty. It's also a lesson in humility. So, the question I pose to nonprofit fundraisers is this: do you lead from the front or from behind?

STRATEGIC
FUNDRAISING
GROUP LLC

CHAPTER NINE
Challenges in the World
of Jewish Philanthropy

We are in the midst of an economic boom. The facts are indisputable. Stocks have soared to unprecedented heights and 401(k)s, IRAs and pension funds are flourishing. During the Trump presidency, tax cuts, deregulation, energy independence, restored manufacturing all positively impacted the economy. Prior to the COVID-19 pandemic, unemployment statistics were at all-time lows, corporate earnings were strong, tariff strategies to leverage foreign markets were successful and the president and Congress approved and signed into law new trade deals that are harbingers of future economic growth.

All of this seemed like good news and resulted in generous increases in philanthropy in general, and concomitantly for Jewish philanthropy in the United States. And yet, there are troubling signs ahead.

I was interviewed not long ago by a budding podcast superstar, host of the "Jewish Philanthropy Podcast," Rabbi Dovid Cohen, about future trends in Jewish philanthropy. You can listen to the full interview at https://podcasts.apple.com/us/podcast/jewish-philanthropy-podcast/id1454383330?i=1000461935949. During the podcast, I suggested that we need to address three areas that will adversely affect Jewish philanthropy.

1) Outmigration: California, Illinois, New York and New Jersey are experiencing major outmigration to the states of Florida, Arizona, Texas and Nevada. People are fleeing in droves. For example, Fox News reported that nine hundred people were leaving New Jersey every day. This translates to $1 million in lost revenue per day. This income is not easily replaced.

   Furthermore, even if they don't move, they are remaining longer in warmer climates for reasons such as tax advantages, new social or business relationships and newly developed community ties. Also, as the Baby Boomers age, or reach retirement, they are more inclined to stay longer in the sunbelt and not return to states notorious for traffic grid-lock, a higher cost of living, draconian tolls and a failing infrastructure. The Jewish community and philanthropy will especially suffer in these states as new charitable loyalties and allegiances are forged elsewhere. Jewish donors are taking their money somewhere else. Out of sight, out of mind.

2) Intermarriage: The trend in interfaith marriages in the Jewish world is troubling, as it also impacts Jewish philanthropy. According to the Pew Research Center Survey of US Jews, "The proportion of Jews who say they have no religion and are Jewish only on the basis of ancestry, ethnicity or culture is growing rapidly, and two-thirds of them are not raising their children Jewish at all. Overall, the intermarriage rate is at 58 percent, up from 43 percent in 1990 and 17 percent in 1970. Among non-Orthodox Jews, the intermarriage rate is 71 percent."

   Why is this of concern? Among other reasons, Jewish philanthropy is affected. The concept of *tzedakah* (charity) is a deeply ingrained and integral Jewish value. This isn't meant to denigrate the giving patterns of non-Jews, but to underscore that the giving of charity embedded in Jewish culture will falter.

Charitable diminishment also will occur, as interfaith donors now giving to primarily secular charities replace formerly targeted Jewish charities. And as older donors die, their giving is generally not being replaced by non-Jewish family members with any nexus to Jewish charities. Generations of traditional donors are beginning to shrink away.

3) The Millennial Challenge: Millennials are generally tradition oriented, *tzedakah* inclined, and want to do the right thing. But they are moving away from writing a blank check whose funds were once used at the nonprofit's discretion. These gifts covered operating deficits or annual budgets. Now they are earmarked to projects Millennials consider appropriate. Special requests are often made to give the money to a needy family or program, but not to operations.

Millennials sometimes consider gifts to the general fund as donations to a bottomless pit. As such, they don't find it desirable to send their funds into an empty abyss. It causes CFOs to have *knipshin*s (Yiddish for "agitation") since they need the money for operations and seek unrestricted funds. Millennials, however, want to see the results of their gift giving. This will become more problematic in time. In some cases, restricted funds also can adversely affect third-party funding.

Today, roughly 80 percent of donations are still coming from Baby Boomers and only 20 percent from the Millennials. But twenty years from now, there will be a tectonic shift. The Millennials are catching up fast. Many of them assume new wealth in the financial industry as hedge fund managers, financial advisors and business executives. Their decisions will surely influence Jewish philanthropy.

These are only three of the challenges facing Jewish philanthropy. If you are a Jewish nonprofit, are you ready for the jarring ride ahead?

CHAPTER TEN
Excuse Me, Does Count Dracula Live Here?

Pirkei Avot (*Ethics of the Fathers*) is considered the go-to tool for improving the world. It is an ageless and extraordinary document consisting of sayings espoused by Jewish scholars who lived from 300 BCE to 200 CE and filled the world with their remarkable wisdom. It offers vision and valuable life lessons.

One dictum, in particular, has universal application. In chapter 5, verse 26, it reads, "Ben Heh-Heh used to say: According to the effort is the reward." In the fundraising cosmos, there was never a more accurate truism. You put forth the effort and you shall, indeed, reap the return on your investment (ROI).

The purpose of this essay is to recount a story about one of my efforts to garner rewards in the pursuit of success. Each year the fundraising journey gets increasingly convoluted as mitigating factors such as economic roller coasters, unexpected pandemics and dynamic social and migration patterns evolve and impact sources of funding. My hope is that today's nonprofits are inspired to put in the necessary effort to realize their financial goals.

An important source of income to one institution for which I worked was the annual allocation to our agency by Jewish Federations. Their budget subventions were critical to plugging holes stemming from our operating deficits. This process included organizing data and comprehensive reports with pertinent information about our agency as we related to each federation. Located in Fairfield County, Connecticut, we were accountable to six federation entities located in Bridgeport, Norwalk, Stamford, Westport-Wilton-Weston, Danbury and Greenwich. This process always required late night meetings in each community where we made presentations.

I often rode through little-travelled side roads late at night guided only by a paper map with tiny print. Yes, this was before the era of the GPS, and how, oh how, did we manage? I still maintain to this day that the GPS is the greatest invention to have improved the human condition since the wheel was invented. I would often call my wife late at night during these trips and ask her, "Barb, where am I?" and she would respond, "How should I know?" and then she would help me navigate out of my predicament.

One foggy night in search of the federation office, I managed to get lost in a desolate part of Greenwich. Suddenly, I arrived at a secluded, dark mansion. It resembled a gothic castle more than anything. I was desperate for directions, so I parked my car and made my way down a long and winding path in search of a human.

Unlike the manicured and well-lit landscapes in town, there was nary a light at this mansion. I was guided by a flashlight low on battery power as I sauntered by a lawn garlanded with tall weeds to the front of the house. Hollywood could not have imagined a scarier entrance. The front door was adorned with a massive knocker in the shape of a dark black gargoyle. No doorbell. I lifted the heavy ornamental door knocker, and the door opened with a hideous creak heard only in horror movies. I smelled an awful pungent odor as the door groaned open. I took a quick look inside, and it revealed a sparsely decorated huge hall with a tall dusty staircase leading to a foyer. And, unbelievably, large cobwebs hovered everywhere. That was all my pounding heart could sustain. I bolted back to the car and made my way out of there faster than the Road Runner outrunning Wile E. Coyote.

No one at the federation office could confirm that such a residence even existed, and they had a good laugh at my expense. But what was important was that their allocation committee approved our funding request. Similar results from the other federation entities we visited made these late-night adventures worthwhile. But the visit to Count Dracula's castle will never be forgotten.

This story resonates with me today because it represents the enormous time and intense efforts we put into just one crucial part of our fundraising program: federation funding. And because we served an array of residents from each of those communities, it made our case so much stronger. Often members of these committees knew our residents and visited them as friendly visitors at the Jewish Home. Hence, those late-night ventures to outlying communities were worth the exertion and rewards.

So, to paraphrase Sesame Street, can you *count* on your funding?

CHAPTER ELEVEN
Measuring Success

The last few months of the year are usually a nail-biting time for many industries, especially for merchants and retailers who bank on major earnings in the fleeting months of the year. This also holds true for the fundraising world.

It is believed that as much as 70 to 80 percent of a nonprofit's fundraising dollars come in during this period, but largely if a major effort is made to secure these funds during the last part of the year. So, during this time in nonprofits across the country, plenty of blood, sweat and tears are shed raising crucial funds.

This is how it works: nonprofits make their best case for support following a year in which they can boast positive results. Sharing warm stories that tug at the heartstrings is one way to touch contributors. Another is to share quantifiable measures of success. The question is how to bring these cold numbers to life—paint them with color, excitement and a patina to which folks can relate.

I once traveled to Los Angeles and met two upwardly mobile professionals who were stars in the hedge fund world. Both were polite and accommodating with their time, but they weren't interested in heart-warming stories. They only wanted to see the organization's budget, metrics and the bottom line. Their minds were made up by the time I met them. But no contribution would be forthcoming until they saw our annual report and the numbers.

Another time, I met with a potential guest of honor for a gala. Her significant philanthropy was well known among her pet charities, amongst which we were counted. She hosted my visit in her penthouse apartment, and I can even recall the aroma of the jasmine tea she served. She sat on many boards that welcomed her input, as well as her generosity (of course). But what was impressive was her avid interest in our fundraising efforts. She wanted to learn about our variety of donor giving alternatives because it spoke to her concerns about the need to offer diverse forms of donor involvement. She asked me for the totals and percentages of charitable giving through major gifts, annual fund giving, private family foundations and trusts, major event support, restricted campaign funding, planned gifts such as bequests and grassroots support. I reviewed quantifiable measures that were the basis of her decision to be our guest of honor.

The obvious lesson I learned is that lay leaders, board members and professionals need to divide their attention between human interest stories and metrics. This is the trend of the future, and the future is now. Certainly, Millennials are more focused on budget deficits and units of measurement than previous donors. The enlightened nonprofit will understand the necessity to share this information because, for some philanthropists, it's all about the numbers.

Walking into a solicitation meeting at the end of the year armed with the right facts can dramatically influence donors. Look at it this way: these statistics represent your report card. You are basically sharing your productivity and effectiveness. Also, having an annual report that shows graphs and charts illustrating an institution's fiscal health goes a long way with many supporters. Obviously, every charitable organization is different, but there are similarities in presentation that all charities share.

Let's distinguish between the kind of metrics that donors need and the kind the nonprofit needs to measure success.

As a contributor, I want to see statistical data over time that show growth and expansion or decline and contraction. For example, if it's a school, donors are interested in learning trends over time, how many students matriculated, how many achieved job skills that lead to quality job opportunities, the number of students that went on to higher education, how many children you serve by grade level and so forth. These are only *some* examples of measures donors rank to determine your stages of success.

As a nonprofit, I want to know how many donors are in the database, how many new donors were acquired, how many donors were retained over time, how many lapsed donors were reactivated to give, how many donors upgraded their level of giving and how much you think certain donors will give over their lifetime. These are only *some* examples of metrics the nonprofit needs to ascertain its rate of success.

The metrics you choose may make the difference between success or failure. Go figure!

CHAPTER TWELVE
Mentoring for Success

What came first, the chicken or the egg? This is the age-old question that sages, and the not so sagely, have grappled with over the ages. The question arises when neophytes, starting a career, face the age-old challenge of being considered for a professional position for which they have little or no experience. The novice rightly asks himself or herself, *Well, how do I gain experience if no one hires me?* Good question.

When I pursued my master's degree, a prerequisite to graduating was taking part in an administrative residency program. For one year, I served as an administrative resident at Fairfax Hospital, a 656-bed facility in Falls Church, Virginia, which exposed me to the field of acute care management and hospital administration. The residency was one way to overcome the chicken-and-egg question. Not everyone is so lucky.

In the space allotted me, let me share mini sketches of some senior executives with whom I worked and whose different and yet dynamic styles were part of my professional growth in the field of development. These vignettes may shed light on what it takes to be a mentor and a role model.

Purely as an aside, I should mention that I was one of few Jewish employees in an organization primarily staffed by a white Anglo-Saxon protestant population. I wore my kippah (Hebrew for "yarmulke") proudly (as I did throughout my career), and in return was treated with respect and dignity. My preceptor, Mr. Rupp, was the executive vice-president of the facility, and I will never forget his coming by my office on Friday afternoons and telling me, "It's almost Shabbos (the Sabbath). Time to leave." Mr. Rupp was not Jewish.

Mr. Rupp was my mentor at the hospital, and I credit some of my success to his regularly taking time to mentor me. Even though this was not the sole purpose of my residency, he introduced me to the foundation office responsible for raising major funds for Fairfax Hospital. It opened my eyes to the essential nature of fundraising in a nonprofit environment. The funds they raised underwrote the CAT scanners, biomedical laboratory, nuclear medicine department and other vital services.

When I moved to Connecticut and worked at The Jewish Home for the Elderly in Fairfield, Connecticut, my mentor was Dennis J. Magid, then executive director. Starting as the director of volunteers and community relations, it was my responsibility to coordinate programs by the women's auxiliary that raised hundreds of thousands of dollars for the facility, and later millions for the 120-bed addition we built.

Dennis was an outstanding administrator, and he lived and breathed fundraising. He involved me in the auxiliary's annual spring luncheon when more than eight hundred women attended at the most beautiful venues. We held mid-summer events such as a reception for one thousand patrons at the Shakespeare Theatre in Stratford, Connecticut, major raffle/dinner-dance programs and an October Ball at the local country club. Mentoring meant supervising me, but also giving me responsibilities ranging from event coordination to recruiting benefactors.

As the executive director/chief development officer at Metropolitan Jewish Geriatric Foundation in Brooklyn, New York, my responsibilities ranged from capital campaigns to annual giving activities to planned giving programs. The mentor who counseled and advised me on the best ways to approach our board was Eli S. Feldman, President/CEO. Eli delegated fundraising duties to me, but also was instrumental in helping me initiate annual golf events that became huge fundraisers. Meeting with Eli, a business entrepreneur by nature, was always valuable because his advice came from a profit-making perspective helpful in strengthening our fundraisers into profit-oriented enterprises.

At OHEL Children's Home and Family Services in Brooklyn, New York, my mentor was David Mandel, a CEO who understood the value of charitable giving. He realized that donations often made the difference whether a program survived or expanded. Recognizing that lead gifts as well as ongoing contributions both added up, was integral to our success. We held regular meetings to discuss the best way to go about securing major gifts, coordinating special events and organizing a panoply of giving opportunities. Having his confidence and trust were key ingredients to his mentoring approach. I appreciated that.

I am forever grateful to the senior executives who mentored me during my tenure with them. They were always forward looking, and they expanded my horizons in the field of philanthropy and in leadership development, an important cog in the wheel of fundraising.

So, my question to professionals today is this: do you have a mentor, or a tormentor, who encourages your path to success?

CHAPTER THIRTEEN
Successful Fundraisers:
Just Luck or Something Else?

Beginning in 1966, the annual Labor Day Jerry Lewis Muscular Dystrophy telethon raised upwards of $2.5 billion. During its forty-five-year life span, it became a staple of regular TV viewing highlighted by a parade of celebrities who joined "Jerry's Kids" to entertain viewers and ask for contributions. Jerry used to say he would be happy if he raised just "one dollar" over the previous year. Yet, he managed to raise quite a bit more. Was it luck or something more?

Luck or maybe something else?

A few years ago, Jeanette Senerchia, whose husband was diagnosed with ALS, also known as Lou Gehrig's Disease, first took what became known as the Ice Bucket Challenge, but did not know what she was about to unleash. Soon the very act of dumping a bucket of ice on your head as a means of raising funds became an overnight viral sensation. It also raised the consciousness of the world and helped scientists discover a new gene tied to ALS. It raised $115 million in 2014, the year it was introduced.

Luck or maybe something else?

The late Rush Limbaugh, the well-known conservative radio personality, decided to support the Tunnels to Towers Foundation by selling a t-shirt with the original Betsy Ross flag on it. The foundation primarily raises money to pay off the home mortgages for families of military, law enforcement or first responders who were either severely injured or killed in action. Limbaugh raised more than $5 million for this project, just an amazing response. After all, we're talking t-shirts!

Luck or maybe something else?

The list of such fundraisers is limitless. The thirty-ninth annual Chabad Telethon raised nearly $4 million for their good work on the West Coast. Different Jewish communities around the United States generously support the United Jewish Appeal (UJA) and Jewish Federation Super Sunday fundraisers, which have a history of raising major dollars. According to 3 CBS Philly, Super Sunday once was the Philadelphia Federation's largest fundraiser of the year raising upwards of half a million dollars. The *Cleveland Jewish News* reported at one point that the Jewish Federation in Cleveland raised $1.1 million on Super Sunday. And, according to Florida's *Sun Sentinel*, the Greater Miami Jewish Federation raised more than $500,000 in pledged donations to the 2018 Federation/UJA Campaign on Super Sunday.

Luck or maybe something else?

How do they raise such large sums of money? More importantly, what are the common ingredients for success in big fundraisers? Is it pure luck or maybe something else?

The answer is not complex. All these activities, and so many more, share crucial commonalities to achieving success. Having raised upwards of $93 million for nonprofits, I can easily conjecture as to how and why nonprofits do so well.

First, let's get the luck part out of the way. There is indisputably a trace of good fortune involved. Who could forecast that dumping an ice bucket on one's head would go viral and raise a ton of money? Likewise, who knew that a t-shirt could fetch in the millions? It's only partly luck, right idea at the right time.

Yet, we can learn some valuable lessons from them that apply to any fundraiser. Here are some for starters:

1) Mission: If donors connect with your mission, you win half the battle. The other half is winning their confidence and trust. Accomplishing these two tasks takes time and perseverance.

2) The 6P's: "Proper prior planning prevents poor performance"—this cardinal rule has guided my career. Even activities tinged with luck require sound organizational planning.

3) Timing: The ice bucket challenge began in the summer and helped propel the craziness. Labor Day was always the time for Jerry's Kids. Super Sunday is ingrained in donors' and volunteers' minds; folks expect it each year around February.

4) The *Ma Nishtana* factor (Hebrew for "what is different?" recited during the Passover Seder): When you read this chapter, it may be the wrong time of the year, but the concept applies year round. If your fundraiser has unique appeal, it potentially will be a draw. You may recall the case of Carson King who became a viral sensation when he held up a hand-drawn sign just asking for beer money when he stood on the set of ESPNs "College GameDay." He raised nearly $3 million for a children's hospital in Iowa.

5) <u>Celebrities</u>: Unquestionably, a celebrity asking for money works wonders. Some celebrities who lost homes in some of the California wildfires joined to help others whose homes were destroyed. Stars such as Lady Gaga, Gerard Butler and Ellen DeGeneres raised and contributed hundreds of thousands of dollars to help the cause.

These are only some reasons why such fundraisers fare well. There are many more. If you are planning a mud marathon, or looking to rappel off a building to raise funds, or planning the next Iron Chef cooking competition, keep these lessons in mind. Oh, and the success of the Jerry Lewis Labor Day was anything but luck.

So, do you have good reasons to succeed, or are you just plain lucky?

CHAPTER FOURTEEN
When Humor Isn't Funny

Every good speaker often begins a speech with a funny story or an ice breaker. These are called "attention grabbers," and the idea is for the speaker to captivate the audience's attention so that folks will listen to the *boring* speech. Sometimes the opening is funny, and the speaker achieves his/her goal; oftentimes a joke falls flat, and the speaker just has to move on. But occasionally it backfires, and that is the crux of my essay.

I spent many an evening and weekend speaking to different groups, often at synagogues and Jewish organizations. Speeches that precede an appeal for funds must be poignant, no more than eight to ten minutes long and get to the point quickly to be effective. There is little time to recover from a yarn that bombs. This is why speakers are encouraged to share their joke or humorous anecdote with a test audience (e.g., spouse, friends, colleagues) before making a fatal mistake.

One misfire happened to me, but wasn't obvious at the time.

It took place on a Shabbat (Sabbath, Saturday) in a synagogue where I was débuting a special appeal for a worthy charity. The true story went like this.

We had gathered at a group residence for developmentally disabled adults not long ago to celebrate Jacob's birthday. Jacob was a ninety-year-old psychologically disabled man hampered with bipolar disorder who was admitted to the residence after many years of institutional living elsewhere. He was a pleasant, likable, trim, gray-haired and neatly dressed man who received support, both personal and medical, and guidance in all aspects of living by the devoted staff. But he had, unfortunately, endured many agonizing hospitalizations in his life because of his bipolar disorder.

Two huge birthday cakes were carved up at his party for the many well-wishers—volunteers, staff and board members—who came by to wish Jacob well on his milestone. Other than an eighty-five-year-old brother who rarely visited, Jacob had no other family. Therefore, the staff at the group residence was his family.

At his party, a proclamation was read by a local politician who designated that day in Jacob's honor. You should have seen his Cheshire smile.

During the program, one person after another got up to laud and toast Jacob. Finally, at the end of the ceremony, one of the residence managers stood up, turned to Jacob and exclaimed, "Jacob, everyone here had something nice to say about you on your ninetieth birthday. What do you have to say for yourself?"

And without missing a beat, Jacob turned to the crowd and declared, "What can I say? Get me a rich widow!"

The story got polite laughs, and we forged ahead with the appeal. But then the feedback coursed in after services. It turned out there were a handful of women in the audience who, as luck would have it, were wealthy widows. They didn't find the story amusing. The fallout wasn't pretty.

Some of the lessons to be learned from this experience are as follows:

- Always know your audience. It helps to identify who is sitting in front of you, information you can get from your hosts. They will likely share who will attend the presentation and can guide you.
- Be humble, and own up to it. No excuses. It never pays to be defensive or try to explain why poor taste is appropriate. Remember this: it's like customer service. "The customer is always right. And when the customer is wrong . . ." Well, you can fill in the blank.
- Remember how you get to Carnegie Hall? "Practice, practice, practice." Rehearse your story or joke with a trusted friend or family member. Getting their feedback might avoid embarrassment.

There is an expression: "Be comfortable with being uncomfortable in order to succeed." Anticipate times when humor fails you, and when it does, you must suck it up and just lumber ahead. "The show must go on." Enough with the clichés.

There are times that humor is simply inappropriate such as when giving a eulogy. And, yet, I remember one speaker at a funeral recounting the funniest moments in the life of the deceased, putting me and the audience in stitches. I never laughed so hard. But it takes a unique talent to carry out such a feat.

Keep in mind: being funny when making a speech is hard for many to pull off. So, I ask you, when was the last time you told a joke?

STRATEGIC
FUNDRAISING
GROUP LLC

CHAPTER FIFTEEN
Who's in Charge of the Chicken Coop?

Having been in fundraising for more than four decades, I feel it incumbent to periodically raise issues that oftentimes might not suit everyone, above all fundraising professionals.

The Association of Fundraising Professionals (AFP) has a Code of Ethical Standards that members, and even those that are not, should adhere to and fulfill their ethical, moral and professional obligations. The first standard reads that "members shall not engage in activities that harm the members' organizations, clients or profession or knowingly bring the profession into disrepute." In its Donor Bill of Rights, it adds that contributors are "to be assured their gifts will be used for the purposes for which they were given." Even if you are not a member of the AFP, every fundraising professional must subscribe to these principles. It's common sense and common decency.

There are an estimated 1.6 million registered nonprofit organizations in the United States, and, like any statistical sampling, there are bound to be bad apples in the bunch that care not about these precepts. The vast majority of nonprofits, however, are true to their mission and rightly deserve the public support they receive. But this chapter is not about them. Instead, it's about the troubling few that make headlines and tarnish the rest of the field. They are the Bernie Madoffs in the field of development.

The CEO of any nonprofit always must be on the alert for greedy persons in his or her midst. Regrettably, there are instances when even senior executives are problematic, and then it is the board of directors that must exercise its fiduciary and oversight responsibilities. Often an audit committee can root out troublesome evidence and uncover illegal, immoral and/or unethical behaviors. It may even require a forensic audit to unearth the truth.

Early in my career as a nursing home administrator, I faced a dilemma. While it's a different field than fundraising, it is useful to share common concepts. Sometimes it takes strong measures to uncover the truth. We once had experienced two serious problems that many nursing homes face: First, linen items were being pilfered. Our facility established par levels, which meant we knew how many sheets, bedspreads, pillowcases and all linen items were needed daily. We kept seeing these levels disappear, suggesting someone was walking off with the goods.

A second problem we faced was the theft of resident personal belongings. This was especially troubling because, when a loved one is entrusted in your care, you must always remain vigilant on their behalf. This matter required urgent and immediate attention.

We passionately debated what to do, consulted with the police and our board and decided to bring in a plainclothes officer to expose the perpetrators—extreme times, extreme measures. Ultimately, we discovered two individuals spiriting out linen items from the receiving dock where no closed circuit TVs were available. We also detected one individual on a night shift rummaging through resident rooms, and caught her leaving with residents' property. The pilfering and theft ended, and management and families were pleased with the results. Word got out quickly about the corrective measures we had taken, and there was great understanding and relief. The problems subsided.

Unfortunately, there have been well-publicized times when even individuals in positions of authority at a nonprofit have misappropriated or misused charitable funds. Nonprofits, therefore, must guarantee that donations are used for their intended purpose.

In March 2016, it was reported that Wall Street hustler Andrew W. W. Caspersen scammed the Moore Charitable Foundation out of $25 million as part of a fraudulent investment scheme. In July 2016, the Leonardo DiCaprio Foundation was part of a $3-billion Malaysian embezzlement scandal. The Kids Wish Network, and others which sound like the Make-A-Wish Foundation but aren't, raised big dollars and spent only 1 to 2 percent, raising questions about where the rest of the money went. Let's understand that these problems occasionally stem from those in authority raising funds.

So, what to do?

Robust security measures ought to be considered. The best advice is only hire individuals in key positions who go through vigorous background and reference checks. Nonprofits also should conduct regular audits of their funding usage. Finally, watchdog agencies such as GuideStar and Charity Navigator that rate and actively monitor nonprofit fundraising should be regularly consulted.

So, my question is this: do you care enough about how you spend your own money? Then you should care enough about how your charity spends theirs.

STRATEGIC
FUNDRAISING
GROUP LLC

CHAPTER SIXTEEN
Are Rules of Thumb for the Dumb?

The Merriam-Webster dictionary defines a rule of thumb as follows: (1) a method or procedure based on experience and common sense, (2) a general principle regarded as roughly correct but not intended to be scientifically accurate. The first known use of a rule of thumb is circa 1658 and not a recent development.

Here are some you may hear every so often:

> "Never stare a gift horse in the mouth."
> "When life deals you lemons, make lemonade."
> "When birds start perching on the lawn, it's time to
> mow it."

And I am sure you can produce many more. Are there truths to be learned from them? Sure. But as the saying goes, "they're not etched in stone."

There is one rule of thumb a graduate school professor of mine shared that is timeless and of great import here. And I sincerely do believe it holds up to the test of time.

His rule of thumb is a well-known universal axiom, one that I know not only makes good sense, but is a directional arrow every fundraiser should faithfully follow. It's the 6P's rule, and, as mentioned before, it goes like this: proper prior planning prevents poor performance.

What I like about this rule of thumb is that it serves as an inner compass to guide you in your work, as a fundraiser and no matter what line of work you do. Let's be frank. If you don't make the effort to properly plan or prepare for a special event or related activities, don't expect great results.

A wonderful mentor I once had was Dennis J. Magid, the president/CEO of an exceptional long-term care facility in Fairfield, Connecticut. Dennis was a brilliant fundraiser and a very successful CEO. He always reminded me when we went into a board meeting that, if you've done your homework well, then you will have written the minutes of the meeting before you walk in. He was right.

I worked with another senior executive who was intimately involved in the seating of fourteen hundred guests at our annual gala. While we worked with a knowledgeable team, he took the ultimate responsibility for situating every guest at every table in the banquet hall, and his work was flawless. This is a serious project, and you can understand that there is little margin for error, especially when some guests can be very sensitive as to where they are seated. Planning this properly is a priority.

Let me be more specific. Planning special events are never last-minute affairs. We do not suddenly sit down and map out the detailed coordination of a major gala the day, week or month before the event. At a minimum, such an affair requires six to eight weeks of planning and likely a three-month campaign from beginning through fruition. There are a host of details to attend to including, but not limited to, save-the-date notices, invitations, site choice, catering, honorees, awards, program, publicity, couvert pricing, sponsorships, entertainment, audio-visuals, supplemental fundraising activities and the list goes on.

Times have changed, and doing things a certain way just because we always did them so—or following "Tradition," as the song in *Fiddler* goes—no longer holds water. I recall attending endless committee meetings to prepare for a major event. Today, most folks don't have the patience, time or energy to hold constant meetings with committees. In some cases, the organization's development staff go at it alone; in others, lay leadership handles the details; and then there is everything in between.

What is important is that adequate planning occurs to develop the strategies needed to assure a successful affair. If you cross all your t's and dot all your i's, you can generally expect to achieve your financial goals. In some cases, there are other goals you can accomplish, and these include marketing and public relations goals, artistic and aesthetic goals to showcase the organization.

What holds true when planning a special event applies in other instances as well. For example, when working a major gift, the fundraiser must do sufficient research about the background of the individual being approached. Knowing a philanthropist's giving history, interests, likes, dislikes and so on generally helps result in a successful pledge. When conducting a direct mail campaign, it always helps to examine other nonprofits' successful campaigns and learn from their experiences. The 6P's rule is applicable in many areas of our lives.

So, do you think rules of thumb are for the dumb? I say, "It is what it is."

CHAPTER SEVENTEEN
Are Sit-Down Dinners a Thing of the Past?

For many nonprofits, the biggest money maker of the year is the annual dinner or gala. Depending on the size of the fundraiser, its history, its philanthropic base of support and related variables often will dictate its financial success. For the purposes of this chapter, we will focus exclusively on the dinner type of gala.

What concerns me is the format of the dinner. Many nonprofit organizations have a tradition of greeting guests with anything from a tamped-down reception, all the way to a lavish smorgasbord or cocktail hour, followed by a sumptuous sit-down dinner during which folks network with one another and listen to a litany of speeches. Usually not memorable ones, I might add. Sorry for the cynicism, but my sarcasm is finely honed after more than forty-five years of listening to stupefying speeches at gala events.

As society has changed, so too must the formats of our dinners if we hope to cling to the donor base that attends these important fundraisers. Today, we live in an age of the sound bite. Folks no longer have patience to listen to hours of talking heads. Closely watch guests at the average charitable dinner. More times than not, they are focused on their smart phones reading texts, emails or even playing Candy Crush. Some politely hide their device under the flap of the tablecloth so as not to be so obvious. But you can tell. And it's true for Baby Boomers as well as Millennials.

New guests are likely there because someone did a little arm twisting, they came to honor an awardee or both. Loyal donors always will attend. Galas are a wonderful opportunity to attract and retain new donors, but nonprofits are losing an opportunity because of the oftentimes built-in tedium created by the program. You might find some of these folks, and loyalists, outside the banquet hall during speeches because they have heard it all before, while the masochists politely stay inside.

I cannot overemphasize what many donors told me about dinners that dragged on and on. It was not unusual for me to hear these declarations: "Let me write you a check and spare me the dinner," or "I will give you a donation but don't make me go, *please*," or "I have heard it all before, so you don't need me there." What some nonprofits do not realize is that numbers have influence and a good showing builds fundraising momentum, while a poor attendance can have adverse consequences. People like to hop onto the bandwagon of winners, not losers.

There are steps nonprofits can take to reclaim their vaunted dinner status of years past. However, they must be willing, *truly willing*, to try new formats that will satisfy their changing donor base.

Here are some ideas to consider:

1. Program length needs to be reevaluated. Why test your guests' patience and sitting comfort? Two hours or more of speeches are not welcome by your donors. Take my word for it. Choose the two to three folks that must speak, and stop. Try to limit your honoree presentations to two to three. Time your program, and keep speeches to three minutes maximum each.

2. Change the dinner format from a sit-down to a different style. For example, have an extended reception followed by a theatre-style sit-down for the short presentations. Obviously, you need a venue that accommodates such configurations.

3. Entertainment, entertainment, entertainment—make it an enjoyable evening. Bring in a celebrity singer, a choir or a mentalist or magician. Let it be a memorable event, not one forgotten before the next day.

4) Consider cutting out the dinner and just have a fun dessert hour. Make the time for your awards right after, and let folks go home early. Your donors will thank you.

5) Arrange for a professional master of ceremonies to navigate the program for you. Most TV or radio personalities such as news anchors or reporters understand the value of a sound bite. They know how to MC because they do it every day. Don't be surprised when the anchor takes your call. They often do. It looks good on their resume, too.

6) Film your honoree responses in advance. There are few exceptions to this rule. Honorees often dictate the financial success of your event. But giving them a few minutes on videotape controls the timing and can only enhance the affair. Use honoree videos to limit their time speaking. And do not have them speak on top of the film.

Dinners are here to stay for the foreseeable future, but traditional sit-down dinners are on their way out. How you change the format will decide whether your donors groan or cheer your decision. Are you ready to stand up and make the right choice?

CHAPTER EIGHTEEN
Board of Directors:
Roles and Responsibilities,
PART I

I was asked by a reader of my newspaper columns whether I would write about working with boards of directors of Jewish nonprofit organizations. It struck me that this individual differentiated between boards of Jewish and non-Jewish organizations. In my view, there is *no* difference, especially if the roles and responsibilities of board members are clearly delineated. Any board normally follows the same principles of governance, advocacy and philanthropy.

The underlying implication raised about Jewish nonprofit boards really is the under-the-surface meaning. Many folks are concerned that these boards are tougher and more challenging to work with than other boards. Having seen other boards in action, it is not the ethnicity or religion that dictates its toughness. Instead, it is its steadfast resolve to succeed by following generally accepted best practices.

Over the years, I worked with both large and small boards. Size is not a determinant of effectiveness. What stays critical is whether boards unambiguously understand their roles and responsibilities. To better understand what this means, let us consider history.

The crucial role of a nonprofit board has increased over time. In 1940, there were only 12,500 charities registered with the IRS. Today, there is an estimated 2.3 million nonprofit organizations operating in the United States, with approximately 1.6 million registered with the IRS. Since 2000, we have seen a nearly 30 percent increase in such entities.

With the explosion of nonprofits, a board's central role in finances, accountability, compliance and transparency has evolved. As a result, over time, more authoritative entities are vigilantly watching nonprofits. These include various state legislatures; the IRS; watchdog organizations such as Charity Navigator, GuideStar and the Better Business Bureau Wise Giving Alliance; the news media; other federal agencies and the public at large including donors. It became apparent that boards needed to be focused on three key areas of responsibility: (1) governance, (2) advocacy and (3) philanthropy.

Board members are the fiduciaries of the nonprofit institution, and govern by steering the organization towards a sustainable future by adopting sound, ethical and legal governance and financial management policies, as well as by making sure the nonprofit has adequate resources to advance its mission.

Board members are uniquely positioned to be successful advocates and ambassadors for their missions. As business leaders, community volunteers, philanthropists and opinion leaders, they have the connections, the confidence and the respect needed to speak up on behalf of their organizations when policy decisions are made that might affect the organization's ability to achieve its mission.

When it comes to philanthropy, nonprofit boards have two indispensable requirements: to give, and to get. This fundraising responsibility is often the most challenging for boards. So, the question often asked is, "Why is this so important?" The answer is simple: giving, and giving generously, ensures that each board member has skin in the game. Personal giving also sets the stage for engaged fundraising by board members.

Experience and research have shown that personal giving by board members works in at least three ways: (1) It is a public declaration that the board member has invested in the charity, (2) It indicates that board members have a commitment to the organization and its mission, and (3) It encourages other donors to give, and impresses institutions that provide grants or other support. In fact, many major donors and foundations will not support a charity unless the board achieves 100 percent giving.

The chief focus of my regular columns is fundraising, and here is why. In 2015, nearly $375 billion were raised by nonprofit organizations in this country, and this was topped by a historic near $450 billion in 2019. These came about primarily vis-à-vis individual donors and major gifts, foundation giving, charitable bequests and corporate giving. It is undeniable that boards of directors played a vital role in raising these funds.

More than fifteen years ago, I took part in a seminar entitled "Building a Fundraising Board." One of the presenters described twelve types of boards. Space limits this conversation in this chapter, but I will address it in the next chapter. Nonetheless, it is irrefutable that if the roles and responsibilities of the board are explicitly defined, then the nonprofit—Jewish or non-Jewish—will be far ahead of the game.

Is your board ready to undertake its mission?

STRATEGIC
FUNDRAISING
GROUP LLC

CHAPTER NINETEEN
Board of Directors:
Roles and Responsibilities,
PART II

In the last chapter, I delineated the roles and responsibilities of *all* boards of directors, regardless of ethnicity or religion. In a nutshell, all boards should adhere to the accepted principles of governance, advocacy and philanthropy (the latter of which means to *both* give and get). Refer to my blog at ngildin.tumblr.com for more specifics.

Ronald Larose, an eminent fundraising consultant, presented a seminar entitled "Building a Fundraising Board" more than fifteen years ago wherein he described twelve types of boards. In my experience, I have come across every version. Let's discuss the *grim* realities.

First, there's the "Some Do and Most Don't" board. This type of board may have twelve to eighteen members on it, but philanthropy (giving and getting) is limited to three to four members who have the capacity to do good. Unfortunately, the burden of carrying the ball falls on the shoulders of these few, which doesn't portend well for the nonprofit.

Then there is the "We Have Never Done This Before" board. *Oy vey!* This type of board may have well-intentioned folks serving on it, but members have no resource development history or philanthropic capacity. The nonprofit won't stand a chance to evolve and grow, because its finances and fundraising future are limited.

The third type is "I'm Not a Fundraising Type of Guy" board. There may be folks here with philanthropic ability, but they have no desire or willingness to undertake their fundraising duties. It is hard to make forward progress unless one can change these board members' inclinations.

The "All Aboard" board is a large group—maybe forty-five to fifty members—with twelve to fifteen proactive donors and ambitious people. Certainly, it benefits the organization having active board members, but the larger group needs specific development guidance.

Some nonprofits have the "Not Quite Prime Time" board with a heavy concentration of mid-level corporate and community leaders. These folks have great potential, but can use leadership training to help them maximize their potential.

A sixth board is the one with "A Good Talent Pool." This is a desirable board to have because there is a good mixture of balanced talent distributed to working committees, with fundraising consigned to a specific committee.

Of course, many of us are quite familiar with the "No Dinero" board. You will often hear them say, "We give our time and talents," and have respectable people on it. But they don't give! Not helpful because a balance of giving and talent is essential.

You may have seen the "An Evening of Reruns" board. This board is constituted of the old guard who describe themselves as "tired and tapped out." Usually, they have no term limits and, historically, have a noticeable absence of younger members.

Senior executives are very acquainted with the "What Kind of Wood Are We Using for the Fence" board. This is a board that exists to oversee the staff and, quite often, micromanages the organization. Frankly, if you hire a competent professional and competent staff, this type of board can be quite counterproductive to the best interests of the organization.

Then there is the "My First Commitment is to My Alma Mater" board. The allegiances and loyalties of this kind of board are questionable. They seem to make other institutions the priority and not the one on which they serve. So, my question is this: what motivates them to serve on the board of this nonprofit in the first place?

Another group is comprised of "Who is in the Driver's Seat Anyway" board. This nonprofit may have a board of directors *and* a board of trustees, or two distinct groups representing different communities and, hence, different constituencies. Again, allegiances may cross swords and not be helpful.

Finally, there is the "Devoted to Playing Small Ball" board. Here you find individuals who love to support special events, which are often labor intensive, or not great on the ROI (return on investment), but do not get involved in major gift solicitations or other indispensable fundraising building blocks. This group also needs direction to set their priorities.

So, which board are you, and are you prepared for change?

CHAPTER TWENTY
Branding: Time for Nonprofits to Learn from Donald Trump

This is not a politically driven essay. However, as a fundraiser, I have been confronted over the years with nonprofits that conveyed a multiplicity of branding messages to donors, and I fear this hindered whether a donor chose one charity over another. So, the purpose here is to cut through the smoke and mirrors.

Let's start with the premise that good marketing and advertising complement fundraising efforts. When a nonprofit is highlighted in various marketing strategies, it generally shines a positive light on the organization. When suitable marketing efforts feature the needs, services or accomplishments of the nonprofit, it adds to the colorful paint palette needed to make the charity more attractive in the eyes of donors. It can only help.

The problem facing many nonprofits is that they like to parade a litany of programs or services, which tends to dull the minds of donors. This is not to suggest that these aren't important or even critical services, but it creates clutter in their minds when a single, clear message is all that needs to get through.

In 1984, a little-known former manicurist and character actress by the name of Clara Peller rose to national, nay international fame, at age eighty-one with her far-reaching "Where's the Beef" advertising campaign for the Wendy's fast-food restaurant chain. Everywhere you went, her branding was in full swing. The advertising agency that produced this trendy catchphrase helped Wendy's generate huge sales—the exact meaning of successful branding. She cut through all the chatter by competitors, and branded the restaurant chain in the minds of consumers. It is well known that when Clara died and the campaign ended, Wendy's went through a severe sales slump.

I also call this approach to branding The Goodyear Blimp method. When you look up at the sky and see the Goodyear or Fuji blimps, the branding for both companies is reinforced. It is an excellent way to cut through the clutter of competitors and solidify the products sold by corporate America in the minds of consumers. These advertising blimps, which are often featured on television, at sports events above stadia or even soaring above overcrowded beaches, are designed with the intention of branding products with the masses.

This brings us to President Trump. Whether you like him or not, the genius of his "Make America Great Again" campaign slogan continues to reverberate even now with his constituency base. It is indisputable that his branding campaign resonated with tens of millions of Americans who liked this message. His more updated motto for the 2020 election of "Keep America Great" charmed many in the middle class just as effectively as MAGA. Political campaigns are often won or lost depending on the efficacy of a catchy mantra or jingle. Of course, it didn't help him overcome the Biden basement strategy in 2020.

So, what are the lessons to be learned from a successful branding campaign?

- Don't try to confuse donors by converging an array of services and programs. You always will have opportunity to focus on individual services, albeit at the right time. But, if in your marketing and advertising you spend time and space clustering a list of your services, keep in mind that this tactic may puzzle donors about your mission and detrimentally impact fundraising.

- Keep your mission statement simple. Use the KISS method. Don't overwhelm people with quantity; impress them with quality.
- Pictures *are* worth thousands of words. The founder of a well-known nonprofit whose pictures always feature a bald child once told me, "There is no mistaking who we serve." The poignancy of these pictures always touches the heart.

Certain themes project strong appeal with donors. I worked for an amazing nonprofit that served many needs: chronically ill elderly, hospice patients, nursing home patients and residents, folks suffering with Alzheimer's type of dementia and other disabilities. I made a deliberate decision to spotlight the terminally ill. Our fundraising efforts were on target, because many folks were emotionally touched by this group or could relate to family who needed hospice care. When it was appropriate, I would shift attention to the elderly, Alzheimer's patients or children. This also is why organizations such as the American Cancer Society, American Heart Association or Wounded Warriors are successful. Their focus is not dispersed among many causes. It is cause centric.

So, when you consider your marketing and fundraising campaigns, think of a clean, simple message that will brand your organization. Perhaps you can work with a company that specializes in branding.

Are you ready to find the beef?

STRATEGIC FUNDRAISING GROUP LLC

CHAPTER TWENTY-ONE
Changing the Organizational Climate into a Fundraising Culture

When trying to change the organizational climate into one of a fundraising culture, it often requires significant changes at the very top of the organizational ladder. The board and the chief executive play the most crucial roles in changing the culture mindset.

This book has a chapter that addresses the different types of boards (see chapter entitled "Board of Directors: Roles and Responsibilities, Part II"). Clearly, it takes a proactive fundraising board chairperson or president, with a down-to-business senior executive, to shift the philosophy of board members from a passive "Someone else will take care of it" state of mind to a "We can do it" mode. When the board is committed to philanthropy and promotes a "give and get" philosophy, fundraising usually blossoms and good things tend to happen.

I have been involved with nonprofits for more than four decades where, in some cases, the boards and the chief executive lived and breathed fundraising. In other instances, I also witnessed boards and executive teams where one or both showed an indifference to fundraising but, at least, were not hostile to raising money from donors and prospects.

One organization in which I was engaged launched a major capital campaign. After setting up a campaign cabinet, I met with a past president of the organization, a member of the fundraising cabinet, whose generosity and contacts would be important to the success of our campaign. I related to him the importance of his participation as a donor, as well as the support we expected from his contacts. His response was, "Norm, I am a volunteer—a nobler endeavor than fundraising." Obviously, changing the culture there was necessary.

A cheerful and positive outlook must emanate from the chief executive and the board, and permeate the organization. Staff and volunteers will then likely understand the importance fundraising has on the bottom line and what is in it for them. They should feel a personal stake in a strong fundraising program. As such, changing the culture won't be difficult. In fact, their involvement can provide a springboard for multiple opportunities to enhance the development program.

When the senior executive isn't fully sold on the *essential* nature of raising funds, it may take more time to invest him or her, as well as board members and staff in the process. This is an example of when certain steps are needed to effect a change in the culture. Often the key is for them to understand how marketing and public relations interrelate to the development program and how one enhances the other.

The chief executive must understand the need for a vibrant development program. He or she should be able to elevate the board's interest level and justify to the governing body the value of an effective development function. Other measures also can be taken to change the environment.

Staff and board members should participate in educational programs—workshops or even retreats—led by a fundraising professional. Topics might include rudimentary programs like "Fundraising 101," or "The Fundamentals of Fundraising," "Understanding the Principles in Donor Solicitations" and "How to Increase Your Circle of Donors." These and related sessions frame the foundation for future development activity.

Board and staff meeting agendas should regularly include topics such as progress reports about special events, new money-raising initiatives or fundraising successes. The organizational conversation cannot focus solely on development activities, but should make up selected elements that keep the conversation going.

Social media is an important tool to spread the word not only to the public but also as an internal way of keeping development on the minds of the board and staff. E-newsletters, e-blasts, timely memoranda or announcements concerning galas or special events get around the organization and underscore the importance of these activities. In fact, much of the nonprofits' literature and various organizational communications should promote these events as long as these are not in-your-face communiques.

Other ways to change the culture include involving board members and staff as volunteers in planning direct mail campaigns, solicitations or other development activities. The fundamental question is this: does the concept permeate from the top on down? It must.

Understanding how the financial health and wellness of the organization is strengthened through development successes goes a long way to inspiring everyone to feel they have a personal stake in promoting the fundraising program.

So, is your nonprofit ready for climate change?

CHAPTER TWENTY-TWO
Charity Watch: Caveat, Emptor

Bestselling author Frank Abagnale, formerly a famed con artist, released a book *Scam Me If You Can*. His book describes charity scams, among others, and how to avoid them, especially at the end of the year when charity appeals abound. The movie "Catch Me If You Can" starring Leonardo DiCaprio is based on the "scamploits" (my word) of Abagnale.

According to Giving USA 2020, Americans donated nearly $450 billion in philanthropic contributions in 2019. What a wonderful and charitable people we are! Yet, this enormous generosity also opened the door to abuse.

Holiday time is the season for nonprofits to reach out to donors and ask for donations. Many organizations bring in as much as 70 percent of their revenue in the last two or three months of the year. Many businesses also find that the last quarter is their make-or-break time.

This also is a precarious time because charity-like predators roam America and plot their sinister intentions. Nefarious crooks prey on innocent donors. Therefore, I declare, "Caveat, emptor," or "Buyer, beware." More to the point, let the donor beware.

Everyone is familiar with the Nigerian prince email that promises a huge fortune. Just mail the prince or his charity a sum of money to redeem your riches. Unbelievably, there are folks that still fall for this scam. As outrageous as it seems, there are trusting folks that take the bait, hook, line and sinker. Sad.

Then, there are the phone calls from kind-sounding telemarketers asking for a donation to the local boys' or girls' club. Some ask you to support the local police benevolent association or some other honest-sounding organization name. Regrettably, gullible folks ante up generous donations without performing their due diligence. It is like pouring your hard-earned dollars into a bottomless pit.

As I was writing this chapter, we were in the midst of hurricane season in Florida. The Bahamas suffered through an unprecedented and destructive storm that laid waste many Bahamian islands. It didn't take long for evil doers to take advantage of the situation and create bogus charities to ensnare the unsuspecting.

Timing is everything, and as we watched heart-wrenching images from the Bahamas, some dug into their pockets and donated to ill-conceived or counterfeit appeals. It happened during the COVID-19 pandemic, as well. Disaster relief sometimes relieves you of your well-intended, but purloined, gifts.

In today's technological age, philanthropists commonly are misled and contribute to non-existent charities. GoFundMe or Facebook sites, and even websites, are created by despicable individuals like the couple that raised hundreds of thousands of dollars for a so-called homeless veteran. All three were charged with theft and conspiracy to commit theft by deception. In some cases, expenses exceed revenues because scofflaws pocket funds.

Fraud is not limited to the Internet. Beware of slick miscreants that look and sound sincere and claim they stand for charities but haven't put into place a 501 (c) (3) not-for-profit organization. There are mandatory steps to create a not-for-profit following established IRS guidelines.

They also must register as a charity in the state where they solicit, and, generally, sham charities don't.

As a donor, give wisely and avoid charity scams. What a shame that authentic eleemosynary institutions that depend on your generosity lose out because of scoundrels who defraud the innocent. So, what steps can consumers take to dodge the unscrupulous?

The AARP compiled a short list of common-sense steps. It's not an exhaustive list, but it is a critical one.

1) Never give in to pressure to make a gift right now. Legitimate charities welcome your gift any time.
2) Beware of the thank-you letter, asking you to renew your gift, with an enclosed return envelope for a donation you didn't make. Fraudsters look for the naïve and gullible.
3) Very few charities give 100 percent of contributions to services. This claim should raise your eyebrows.
4) Check charity watchdogs such as Charity Navigator, GuideStar or the Better Business Bureau's Wise Giving Alliance to ascertain the legitimacy of a charity.
5) Research the charity; learn whether it does what it says.
6) Be wary of charities whose name or website mimics real ones.
7) Never offer personal information such as birthdate, social security number or bank account numbers. These are prime for misuse.
8) Contribute using a credit card or check. They have built-in safeguards.
9) Never assume that pleas for help on social media are legitimate.
10) Be careful when clicking on links. These can unleash terrible viruses, ransomware or malware that can purloin your private

financial information, and even hold you hostage until you give in to their perverse demands.

What we don't want are folks holding back and not giving to those genuinely in need. So, when donating, I ask you, do you want to help victims, or do you want to become one?

CHAPTER TWENTY-THREE
Do Fundraising Journals
Make Attractive Doorstops?

Fundraising journals do *not* make attractive doorstops. Some are big and clunky. Others are slim and trim and may not even hold the door open. You might even trip on one when walking through the door. Hence, they don't serve a useful purpose.

In case you haven't sensed my sarcasm, I don't like printed journals. Yes, I know. Printers now will hate me. Some nonprofits also will reject this premise. I understand their sentiments, but after years of dealing with the "journal project," I cannot in good conscience recommend a printed journal to any nonprofit. Yes, I know. Some make boatloads of money. I know.

I once worked for a nonprofit where I eliminated the printed journal and successfully substituted a different fundraising choice. After several years, a prominent board member in favor of printed journals got up at a board meeting and read a poem written by his granddaughter. He asked how could I not put this beautiful, poignant poem into the journal. I was nauseous, but his speech was persuasive, and he turned the board around. Regrettably, we returned to the printed journal.

So, you ask, why do I feel so strongly? Here's why.

Printed journals are labor-intensive projects. Keeping track of an assort-ment of sizes, colors and order on the basis of political sensitivities is a project unto itself. However, that's the easy part. What I experienced was having donors call in their ads, many at the last minute, with the following request: "Why don't you compose something for me?" Staffs always were consumed with creating new prose masterpieces that rivaled the best of Robert Frost, and had to go through countless approvals before final approval. The back and forth alone was time-con-suming and, in my judgment, wasteful.

Then came the proofing process, which was stress driven, especially for last minute donors. And, Heaven forbid, if a sentence, a word or a letter were out of place or omitted, we would never hear the end of it. Or, worse yet, if the ad was inadvertently left out, or misplaced within the book, then it was a cause for corporeal punishment. And if you missed the printer's deadline, oy vey!

This brings me to the cost of printed journals. Oh my God, what a waste of money! Some of these journals cost tens of thousands of dollars. As a donor, I don't want my money to be sunk into an uneconomical sink-hole. I want my money to go to the cause and to the *essential* services of the cause. There are some nonprofits that spend extravagant sums to put in page after page of pictures and other superfluous designs. Yes, some of the information is for marketing purposes. But there are other more efficient ways to market your nonprofit.

Here's what happens after the event. Truckloads of journals are left behind on tables. Few want them and, other than the honorees, some of their family, friends and staff, journals find their way to the recy-cling depot. People no longer want to clutter up their home with printed journals.

There are those that argue that vendors and corporate America need to show printed ads to justify their marketing expense. There are ways to get around this and still meet their needs. So, what are alternatives to the printed journal? There are many not-so-new and, yet, innovative options.

In case you haven't noticed, the trend is to get away from printed journals.

For a few years, the scroll of honor became a popular way to recognize someone in writing without an elongated testimonial. The scroll comes in various formats. Some recognize the donor in the hierarchy of giving, largest gifts first in descending order by donor name. Some scrolls have a sentence or two about the honorees, but no longer replicate *War and Peace*.

Other organizations are taking advantage of putting their journal online, either on their website or with a vendor whose sole business is to display your scroll of honor or journal. By inputting your name, the honoree's name or by typing in the size of donor page, you can go directly to the ad. Others show the ads on a large screen at the event, and make this accessible after the event on a flash drive.

My son Alex and daughter-in-law Shirley were honored at several school dinners. One nonprofit gave everyone a gold key, which was a flash drive that had the ads on it, along with other marketing materials. They also placed digital tablets on all the tables, and guests could easily find and see their ad by using the search function.

There are many other cost-effective and less onerous substitutes to the printed journal. You are only limited by your creativity.

So, are you ready to get rid of your doorstop?

CHAPTER TWENTY-FOUR
End-of-Year Thanks + Giving

"You're late!"

"What do you mean I'm late?"

"If you are only now planning your end-of-year giving campaign, then you are late in getting it off the ground!"

Unfortunately, many nonprofits delay their end-of-year fundraising campaign preparations when the planning for these should ideally start in the summer or no later than September and then get implemented in November and December.

Why?

Year-end giving can often be critical to a nonprofit organization. Here are some eye-popping statistics to keep in mind.

It has been shown that nearly one-third of annual charity donations occur in December. In addition, 12 percent of *all* giving generally takes place in the last three days of December! About 54 percent of nonprofits begin planning their appeals in October, giving themselves unneeded stress because of last-minute planning.

November and December are considered the most popular months to make asks from donors. Almost one-third of nonprofits raise between

26-50 percent of their annual contributions from their year-end ask. About 36 percent of nonprofits raise less than 10 percent of their annual funds from their year-end appeal.

Remarkably, two-thirds of donors do absolutely *no* research before giving. This means they may just instinctively respond to a direct mail appeal without as much as looking at their charity's Charity Navigator or GuideStar ratings. Instead, they may contribute because a family member or friend recommended the charity, or a direct mail piece looked particularly attractive. This is especially startling because we live in an age of technological advances when it is far easier than ever before in history to learn about the validity and cost efficiency of a favorite charity.

Another interesting fact is that volunteers are twice as likely as non-volunteers to give to the nonprofit. This is because, firstly, a volunteer connects more easily with the mission of the nonprofit and usually has a charitable bent to giving. In addition, since it is your volunteer who provides you with a volunteer service, this type of volunteer generally has a special place in his or her heart for your organization. So, hold on to your volunteers because they not only like your cause, but also will likely give to it.

Finally, direct mail is still the most popular medium used to reach donors en masse at year end. E-mail is the second most popular method to reach donors at year end, followed by posting year-end giving information on the organization's website and then personal asks (by phone and in person).

So, what are we to make of this information?

First and foremost, direct mail campaigns still reign supreme. Plan your direct mail campaign carefully, and remember that indicating in your mailings that your donor's gift is *tax deductible* is still critical, so prominently insert it into your literature: e-newsletters, hard copy newsletters, mailing literature of any kind, e-blasts and all fundraising literature.

Donating on your website should be a painless procedure. Check your website to be sure that it does not take forever to open. If it does, then your customers will likely take their business elsewhere. Also, check your donation page fields to be certain they perform as they are supposed to work.

Be sure that your donation page doesn't distract from the job at hand, which is for your contributor to make a gift. Don't distract with other options such as "How about giving a monthly gift?" or "Sign up here to volunteer" or by shifting to the organizational video. Focus, focus, focus on getting the gift; the rest can come later. Remember, this is for end-of-year giving.

Your e-blasts should complement your direct mail pieces. Sometimes these act as replacements or as positive reinforcement to your donors who received the direct mail piece but it got shoved under the pile and was forgotten. These e-blasts should be singular in purpose, as well—a simple message and to the point. In addition, be aware that web campaigns will only increase in the future and will reap increasing dividends over time, if not now.

Finally, carefully plan your phone lists, because making those personal touches at year end—over the phone and in person—will cap off a successful fundraising year.

Is your organization ready for the end-of-year finale? In that case, you may take a bow.

CHAPTER TWENTY-FIVE
Fire in the Belly

This is your "finding the needle in the haystack" chapter.

According to the National Center for Charitable Statistics, there are roughly 1.6 million registered nonprofits in the United States, give or take. The vast majority need ongoing fundraising activities to sustain their programs. Some have the luxury of fundraising staff that raise *essential* funds. In other cases, lay leaders and volunteers spend time raising money. Let's focus on what to look for when recruiting development staff to support a nonprofit's fundraising program.

Newer methods are used to recruit employees today thanks to technological advances. Mobile and online recruiting have made large dents compared to the old-fashioned method of recruiting employees vis-à-vis newspaper classified ads. Word of mouth, of course, is always best.

Finding qualified development staff is often a struggle. I spent thousands of hours over the years reviewing resumes, interviewing contenders, narrowing candidates down and hiring others. I can attest to the fact that finding qualified fundraisers is not easy. In fact, it is downright difficult. Hence, the proverbial "needle in the haystack" analogy.

So, if you are a nonprofit, what do you look for in a development professional? Of course, it depends on whether you are recruiting the chief development officer as opposed to a development assistant. Their job descriptions vary radically, and the goals for each differ. However, allow me to opine that all development professionals share certain characteristics. Let me suggest some.

When choosing a development professional, I use tangible and intangible criteria. A good case can be made to use the same criteria for personnel searches in other industries. True. If it works for you, why not?

Let's examine some tangible criteria first. All are common sense, but let me delineate them.

The first tangible measure is the applicant's resume, or curriculum vitae, which should succinctly depict the person's core accomplishments, professional work experience, years worked, education and other noteworthy information such as special skills, awards, memberships and related pertinent facts. You look for the best fit commensurate with the written job description.

The resume should be concise, to the point, neat in appearance and easy to navigate. I have seen, on many occasions, resumes that required a GPS to circumnavigate. All that was missing was the AAA TripTik.

Next, I look at the applicant's personal appearance, demeanor and communication abilities. Why? Simple. I always look for someone who looks neat, someone with an even temperament, even a keen sense of humor and one who has an ability to properly articulate your mission, services and activities.

How the applicant fares during the interview will ultimately dictate whether he or she moves forward. If the applicant falters in answering specific questions, that is not a good sign. Missteps during the interview include the candidate talking too much, acting incoherently or giving rambling answers, making personal confessions, constantly interrupting or effecting poor comportment. If the applicant fares well, you move on. Receiving a written acknowledgment from the applicant following the interview is always a plus.

A background check is much easier today with a vast array of technological tools at your disposal. You would be shocked at what you can learn from these tools: criminal records, conflicting information contradicting what the candidate presented to you and personal information that you seek but cannot legally ask the applicant. Hooah!

References are the next tangible item I look at. A minimum of three references is suitable. I might look at comments from a supervisor, a lay leader or volunteer or a donor the applicant solicited. Some combination of these testimonials helps give a rounded picture of the aspirant.

Probably the paramount intangible I look for is what we call a candidate's fire in the belly. Very often it is this criterion that could be the most important determinant. Short of some form of abdominal surgery, how does one assess fire in the belly? Not so easy. Here is what I look for: a person's passion and interest in the organization's mission, a personal excitement about what the institution achieves and an eagerness or enthusiasm to undertake the job.

Disqualifiers for the job are easy to enumerate because they are exactly the opposite of what we listed before. Examples might be a messy resume or one that doesn't describe meaningful credentials, showing up late to an interview without a legitimate excuse, inappropriate dress or conduct during the interview, bad references and a lack of fire in the belly. The latter is one of the most important criteria in my view.

So, if you are looking for a qualified development professional, would you prefer someone with fire in their belly, or are you willing to tolerate an inflammation of the gut?

CHAPTER TWENTY-SIX
How About a Night at the Races?

Early in my career, I volunteered for a nonprofit organization that was trying to raise money to meet its daily obligations. When I joined, one of my first recommendations was to form a development committee to address organizational fundraising. It generally helps to ask for the input of the brightest minds around the table whose singular mission is to help the nonprofit. These folks will usually participate in various ways to aid the organization's development efforts.

Along came "How about" Harry. Harry was the volunteer whose help you do not want on a serious and focused committee. Harry usually came up with harebrained schemes that would fall flat on their face. However, Harry was a long-standing board member, himself affluent and influential when it came to persuading others to go along with his ill-conceived ideas. Get me the smelling salts now!

Harry's contribution to meetings went something like this. "How about we have a car wash fundraiser?" This during the fiercest snowstorms yet. Yes, what a great idea to mobilize volunteers to stand in the parking lot in sub-zero temperatures to wash cars in the freezing cold and have cars get dirty as soon as they pulled out of the lot. I kid you not. How about that?

At one meeting, Harry produced this doozy: "How about a night at the races?" This was the game plan. A company he discovered, of course, provided movie reels (this was before the era of DVDs, flash drives or streaming options) that featured previously run horse races that had taken place around the country such as at Pimlico, Yonkers Raceway, the Meadowlands Race Track and elsewhere. The sealed movie reel cans are broken open at the event and each race shown after guests are invited to place bets—show, place and win—at the betting booth we set up. No one presumably knew these horses, or the races they ran, and racetrack programs describing the horses' race histories and related information were distributed to guests on admission.

Keep in mind that the nonprofit had to put up the money from the pot that would presumably be offset by the betting. The time devoted to betting, each race and collection from winnings was about twenty minutes. We were in for a long evening with nine races! Of course, the organization also supplied refreshments for the event. Alcohol would have been a good choice, but the strongest beverage was caffeinated coffee.

Finally, the night arrived, and all the volunteers were mobilized to help in various and sundry ways. Harry was promising attendance by lots of folks, including many of his friends. I had my doubts but, after offering my advice, remained a loyal team player. There just was no stopping Harry. Very little lead time was built into planning and executing the event—perhaps a few weeks to plan, publicize and run the event.

The evening ended with a total of six couples attending. Any bets placed were outstripped by the winnings. So, after a lot of time devoted to this cause, the nonprofit invested many resources to an event that yielded poor results. So, was this a good teaching moment? What did we learn from this fiasco?

There are so many lessons from this affair; where to begin? Let's start with the basic axiom I learned from a grad school professor of mine, the 6P's: "Proper prior planning prevents poor performance." We should seek the input of our board members and volunteers, but we must also think strategically and plan properly if we are to achieve fundraising success. This is why I strongly encourage nonprofits to profit from the wisdom of a strategic fundraising plan.

Space prevents me from describing the elements of such a plan, but suffice it to say that a properly designed plan becomes the roadmap to success for the organization. It is worth the investment of time to construct such a plan so that the nonprofit can follow a path to financial success.

So, are you prepared to gamble at the races, or would you rather ride all the way to fundraising success?

CHAPTER TWENTY-SEVEN
Is Patience a Virtue?

I have always been fond of the saying "Patience is not simply the ability to wait, it's how we behave while we're waiting." Oh, so true! It is often an accurate truism among nonprofits that unrealistically feel that their development director has an uncanny ability to wave a magic wand and raise major funds without having first developed or cultivated relationships with their donors or prospects.

We live in an age of instant gratification. We absorb news in sound bites. We need our instant coffee, *now*. We buy express tickets to avoid lines at Disney, pay for TSA pre-check shortcuts at airports or pay more in HOV express lanes on the Turnpike. We can't arrive fast enough to suit ourselves. Sometimes I think we go through life in three phases: fast, faster and faster than that. *Whoosh*—can you feel the breezy air brush past your face? Some view fundraising the same way.

I once saw an ad by a nonprofit for a director of development position. Next to the ad it read, "Rainmaker Wanted." Well, isn't that special? Wouldn't we all like to recruit a rainmaker to raise lots of money immediately for the nonprofit organization? I harbor serious concerns about this hyped-up hope. Let's examine the issue of patience when fundraising, shall we?

As we head into the robotic age and the era of artificial intelligence, some aspects of our lives will never be controlled by automatons. Fundraisers will still need to interact between humans and their fellow man and woman. I cannot foresee a robot making a personal appeal for a major gift (see chapter called "Fundraising in the Year 2075"). No, robocalls don't count.

Yoav (Job), a well-known Bible character, was said to have unfathomable patience. When someone exhibits great endurance through all kinds of trials and tribulations, annoyances or provocations, we say that person has "the patience of Job." Fundraisers every so often struggle and face a myriad of challenges, especially when asking for major gifts. I spoke a while ago to a colleague who was about to close on a multi-million-dollar gift for an overseas institution of higher learning. He told me that this donation was "five years in the making." The donor, in his 80s, was planning this gift as a legacy for his children, grandchildren and great grandchildren. My colleague let on that this ultimate gift went through many twists and turns over the years, and it wasn't until a recent health scare that he decided the time was right to make the gift. My colleague has the patience of Job.

What also was plain to me was the patience of the nonprofit. It rode the waves with my colleague and factored in that monumental gifts often take time to execute. Of course, in the interim, major gifts were being secured from other philanthropically inclined individuals. They weren't beholden to just one donor. But not every organization has such patience.

Many years ago, I secured a $5 million bequest for one reason alone. I stewarded a board member who had been all but lost to my nonprofit. This lay leader had not been solicited for advice or counsel, and her stature was ignored for many years by the nonprofit's board. She once told me, "Norman, I am ready to take my business elsewhere." Enter a new approach. I made sure that leadership would call her to attend meetings, they elicited her opinion on issues of concern to the organization and she was regularly recognized for her past contributions. It took time, a lot of time, but we won her back, and, once again, she and her family felt like they belonged to the family, in a well-deserved place in the organization.

Winning over an overlooked and ignored board member did not happen overnight. In this case, patience was indeed a virtue. But like all things in life, the relationship took on its own twists and turns. There were times when our neglected board member, whose uncompromising personality often crossed swords with other volatile board members, was ready to bolt. It required tact and diplomacy on a par with a UN statesman to bring her back.

The moral of this story is simple. It often takes time, mental fortitude and physical endurance to shepherd a donor through a major gift process and to keep them in the fold. The effort must be genuine, but is often intense. Understanding this process will usually get you good results.

My question is this: are you willing to be patient, or are you looking for immediate results?

STRATEGIC
FUNDRAISING
GROUP LLC

CHAPTER TWENTY-EIGHT
Is There a Link Between the Economy and Fundraising?

Is there a link between the state of the economy and fundraising? My first instinct is to say, "Yup, you betcha," especially having gone through up and down cycles during the last forty plus years. For example, take the year 2008. Please! That's when the economy started to tank, and many nonprofits saw their fundraising revenue dip.

Let me be very clear. Donors told me during good economic times that's why they gave generously. During lackluster times, donors complained to me why their donations were down. Pretty simple.

But let's stand back and take an objective view to arrive at the correct answer and understand the implications.

In a white paper prepared by Target Analytics entitled "The Macroeconomics of Fundraising," the link is clear.

> The nonprofit sector is not an island . . . It represents about 5% of the economy in the United States . . . The macroeconomic factors that influence the rest of the U.S. economy necessarily influence the nonprofit sector as well, and often have a significant impact on the success—or failure—of fundraising efforts.

Without getting into the weeds, there are generally six factors that influence the level of philanthropic contributions in this country, and they are income, wealth, tax policy, interest rates, unemployment rates and population growth.

Research by the Giving USA Foundation tells us that fundraising dollars received by nonprofits show growth during strong economic upturns and display significant declines when the economy is sluggish. We have seen over time that individual giving is directly linked to their income and wealth. There is a psychology that permeates the economy when incomes rise, and wealth proliferates. When the economy is robust, folks feel a sense of personal security and, thereby, are encouraged to give to their favorite causes.

When the S&P 500 and the stock market have risen, so too have charitable contributions. No surprise here. But what is interesting is that the connection between the S&P 500 and donations is so strong that it is considered by some as the strongest predictor of altruistic gains by the nonprofit sector.

In 1917, Congress introduced the charitable deduction into the federal tax code. Unquestionably, this encouraged widespread investment in private philanthropy. By reducing their tax liabilities, higher income tax earners were encouraged to grant more in charitable gifts. In 1986, the Tax Reform Act proved how tax policy adversely impacted donations when Congress dropped many deductions. The following year, giving from individuals dropped by more than a billion dollars!

Lower interest rates also affect different segments of the population when it comes to giving. For a younger group, lower rates for mortgages, car loans, business loans and the like can be very favorable for nonprofit giving as these folks find charitable ways to invest their money. On the other hand, lower rates can hurt older people whose returns on savings vehicles such as Treasury bills, certificates of deposit and mutual funds grow weaker. Under these circumstances, seniors may give less to the nonprofit sector.

As unemployment rates increase, logically, there appears to be a causative link between people who have less disposable income and the amount of money they give to charity. This doubtless holds true for those seeking employment and those who drop out of the labor force altogether.

Finally, statistical trends point to a shrinking donor pool in the overall population. The pool of possible donors is not as big now as it was a dozen years ago. Part of the reason is that following the "baby boom" of the '50s and early '60s, there was a "baby bust" in the late '60s and '70s. This latter group will enter their fifties in the next ten to fifteen years. So, don't be surprised by dropping donor populations in the foreseeable future.

So, what are the implications of a strong economy and fundraising? Is your nonprofit well organized and prepared to take advantage of the cycle we are in right now? Depending on tax reforms in each session of Congress, nonprofits stand to gain or lose a great deal. It could be a windfall. Is your organization ready?

STRATEGIC
FUNDRAISING
GROUP LLC

CHAPTER TWENTY-NINE
Let's Honor Steven
Spielberg at the Gala!

When in the midst of the vaunted gala season, it is proper to devote this space to what is probably the most challenging yet potentially one of the most lucrative fundraisers for a nonprofit. Let's examine one of the greatest challenges facing nonprofits today: choosing honorees for the special event.

It is a fundamental fundraising principle that honoring the right individual(s) at a nonprofit's gala usually dictates the financial success of the event. If you have done your homework, and researched the folks you wish to honor, then you will likely be financially successful. So, let's consider what we look at when selecting a guest of honor or honorees.

I sat in on many planning meetings when a gala committee member would chime in with gems such as this: "Let's honor Steven Spielberg at the gala! He will be a big draw and will sell a lot of tables and journal ads." After restraining myself from laughing out loud, I asked this question respectfully, "Oh, do you know Mr. Spielberg?" When the answer inevitably was "No," I indicated, "Well, unless you, or someone with whom you are friendly, know him well, really well, and you are willing to ask and secure him as the guest of honor, it is not going to happen."

As sure as the sun rises in the east and sets in the west, this type of question is asked countless times among innumerable nonprofit organizations around the country. The problem is this: an inordinate amount of time is spent on this futile distraction instead of on what is critical, which is identifying and reaching out to authentic prospects that can indeed sell tables and journal ads.

Among criteria we look at before asking worthy individual(s), I suggest the following questions be asked, albeit not necessarily in this order:

1) Do they deserve the honor? There are many folks who demurely defer but, in fact, are capable of drawing donors because they have invested themselves in the organization and *earned* the honor. Also, what a wonderful way to thank such folks.

2) Is there a board member, a volunteer or a donor who distinguished himself or herself on behalf of the organization? Always look close to home first before looking elsewhere.

3) Is there someone with a link to your organization's mission worthy of recognition that everyone will agree makes sense? For example, if your nonprofit deals with children's issues, then selecting a pediatrician or child specialist, someone with name recognition in the field, makes logical sense.

4) Is there a celebrity with whom the organization is genuinely connected who is willing to lend his or her name to the cause? This person should be of noteworthy status, a draw, able and willing to share his or her celebrity standing to attract friends and donors and give willingly of his or her time. At a minimum, they might serve as a high-quality master of ceremonies.

5) I don't wish to sound crass or mercenary, but is the honoree candidate(s) either affluent and/or influential? And, most importantly, are they willing to use their wealth status to, literally, bring peers to the table that also are rich and/or

influential? *Will they make an impact gift?* Face it: folks like this can make the event a financial success.

In my opinion, here are some possible candidates the nonprofit should stay away from when choosing an honoree:

1) Politicians: Let me be candid—no, let me be blunt. Politicians are in it for themselves! Yes, that's right; I said it. They are not usually prepared to solicit their friends or constituents. They fundraise for themselves 24/7. While this is my cynical approach to politicians, it is culled from my observations over many years. Of course, for every rule there are exceptions, and it's no different here. If you have formed a slate of suitable honorees, and you seek some modicum of panache for the affair, then sure, why not? It also might make sense if the politician is embedded within the community with an abundance of friends, family and others who feel indebted to him or her. Constituents and others who are grateful to the politician for his or her positive accomplishments over the years may see this opportunity to say thank you. Fine.

2) Individuals of dubious character: This sounds like common sense, but some nonprofits are sometimes desperate to find anyone, even someone with a scandalous past or even a questionable present. The individual(s) may be very affluent, and this may be why he or she is considered. Nevertheless, the size of a gift is simply not worth tarnishing your reputation or offending constituents.

3) Individuals lacking commitment: These are folks that won't share their prospect list, and/or tell you in advance that they won't solicit anyone or take part in any meaningful way with the gala. But, of course, they would be happy to accept the honor. No, thank you.

4) Egotistical individuals: These are people that you must incessantly plead with to accept the honor. *Never* beg.

There are many topics not covered in this chapter, such as how to make the ask, ways to generate more revenue at the event or even new formats to consider. We will cover these elsewhere.

So, is your organization ready to select its gala honorees, or would you rather watch *Raiders of the Lost Ark*?

CHAPTER THIRTY
The Storyteller vs.
the Number Cruncher

What was your favorite story growing up? My children's favorite book was *The Spooky Old Tree* featuring the Berenstain Bears. My kids would gather around me, or sit on my knee, and what fun we had sifting through the pages over and over again. They would never tire, and I would not tire of reading the book repeatedly.

What was so great about *The Spooky Old Tree*? Well, it encompassed adventure, mystery, suspense, courage, humor and poignancy, and it was an easy read. It had all the captivating ingredients, just like cliff-hangers from the Indiana Jones series. What's important here is that it held our attention until the bears were home again, safe at last.

It's the same way in fundraising. If you can articulate an interesting and poignant story about someone for whom you care or serve, and you can reach into the emotional wellsprings of the heart of the donor, and if it is bona fide, then you stand a good chance of attaining a generous gift. This is generally the case, but times have changed as explained below.

In my experience, there are essentially three approaches to fundraising. The first approach is what I call "The Storyteller" approach; the second is the "Number Cruncher" approach. Both are valid strategies. It's just a question of when you utilize one versus the other, or the third, some combination thereof.

There is a famous saying: "Give a man a fish and you feed him for a day; teach a man to fish and you feed him for a lifetime." This lends itself to The Storyteller approach to fundraising. Let me illustrate.

A nonprofit organization I worked for provided a carpentry workshop for troubled teenagers who were rejected by their families or were homeless. Some were recovering addicts or rehabilitating from trouble they got into while aimlessly wandering the streets.

I visited this workshop and met a young man—let's call him Teddy—who was engaged in crafting bed frames that would eventually be sold in stores. Teddy, a seventeen-year-old Israeli, spoke little English, and when I found him in the workshop, he was fully occupied constructing bed frames. We talked for a while and I asked him why he was there. He told me in broken English, "I cause trouble. I cause trouble." It turns out that his family threw him out of the house, and he roamed the streets for a few years engaged in petty theft, dabbling in dangerous drugs and periodically getting arrested. His life was a mess, and he was close to suicide when the nonprofit found him.

They brought him in from the cold, gave him shelter, food to eat and some good ol' love and nurturing. Before long, he was fabricating dining room chairs, swing sets, picnic tables and beds. Suddenly, he found a purpose in life. He felt wanted, and he was turning out beautiful furnishings that earned him praise and a modest living. He eventually reconciled with his family, felt accomplished, enjoyed a hopeful future and today works in the furniture industry.

Donors felt good when I recounted this story, a genuine tale of turning a young man's life around from crime to one of meaningful accomplishment and success. This real story paved the way to generous gifts.

Then there is the Number Cruncher approach to fundraising. I once visited some hedge fund managers in California. They cared less about Teddy and his overcoming hurdles to achieve triumph. What one said was, "Show me the numbers!" They were only interested in the nonprofit's budget, its operating deficit and organizational metrics. There was no pulling at their heartstrings. They had no time for touching stories.

What lesson is to be learned from this experience? Simple. You need to understand where your donor is coming from and address his or her needs. The emotional approach was of no consequence to my hedge fund friends. Instead, it became purely an exercise in intellectual thinking. Keep this in mind when talking to your philanthropic supporters. Perhaps one approach, or some combination, would be in order.

So, what will it be, *The Spooky Old Tree* or the Book of Numbers?

STRATEGIC
FUNDRAISING
GROUP LLC

CHAPTER THIRTY-ONE
Take Control of Your Event and Make Money!

Here's a startling, if not alarming, fact courtesy of a study done some years ago by Charity Navigator: the average charity spent $1.33 to raise $1.00 in special event contributions. Uh-oh!

Now to utter something sacrilegious, a special or major event is *not* for every nonprofit organization. Uh-oh!

That's right. Not every organization can pull off a gala or major event *and* achieve a healthy profit.

There's a saying: "If you don't know where you are going, then any road will take you there." Unfortunately, too many nonprofit organizations feel that, like the "Fiddler on the Roof" classic, hosting their dinner is "Tradition." So, we must have that annual dinner, right? Wrong! Times have changed.

Dinners and other such major special events are still central to the fundraising efforts of many institutions, but the rules have changed, and getting the right compass or GPS will help guide you on that roadmap to success.

Fundraising events must be treated like a business. Even if your intention is to break even so that you can recruit lots of new friends, or have a friend-raiser, you still need that blend of common sense called "seichel" (Yiddish word for "wisdom") and an astute business acumen so that the major event doesn't *sink* the clichéd *ship.*

No two organizations are alike, so just because your competitor is losing his pants, doesn't mean you have to walk around in shorts, too. Major events can be labor intensive and may not show a good return on the investment. I have always held the belief that securing a $100,000 gift from a major gift donor in one or two meetings is generally more cost effective than sinking in all your efforts for four to five months and only realizing a miniscule gain for your time and labor. Friend-raising is good, but does not have to be all-consuming to the detriment of the nonprofit.

There are specific steps that all nonprofits can and should take to avoid draining their already limited resources if they are determined to host a major event. I am a firm believer in the 6P's (read my chapter entitled "Are Rules of Thumb for the Dumb?"). The planning starts with a budget. Remember math in grade school? Some folks seem to forget that before you secure the hall, hire the caterer or send out one invitation, you must project what your expected revenue and expenses will be. What a novel idea!

If you feel that the net surplus is sufficiently large to catapult your organization into a special event, there are other variables to consider. These include securing the right guest of honor or honorees. I know there are many folks who don't want to hear this, so I urge them to put their ear plugs in right now or just leave the room. Ready? Here goes. *The guest of honor and/or honorees generally dictate the financial success of your affair.* So, as the sagely knight said in an Indiana Jones movie, "Choose wisely."

Other methods to generate income at your event include creating sponsorship levels that recognize donors for different gift elevations;

inserting a special event within the larger event such as a VIP reception so that you can recognize larger gift donors; providing a mobile digital platform for gift giving, especially useful for guests who have not paid the couvert but are coming at the invitation of friends that paid the price of admission, and setting up a matching gift challenge during the affair (this has to be carefully arranged in advance with one or more of your philanthropically generous friends). There are other strategies, but space is limited.

It is understood, but since this is a book that offers advice, superfluous overhead should be eliminated and the best pricing for your amenities should be a priority. An effective publicity campaign should include anything from print advertising to social media. Finally, unpaid pledges cannot be forgotten, so a well-organized collection plan also should be implemented after the event.

If you follow a well-coordinated fundraising plan for your special event that incorporates these types of approaches, then the likelihood for success is high. And not least of all, put the fun back into fundraising.

So, is your nonprofit prepared to take control of your special event and make money?

CHAPTER THIRTY-TWO
The Ethical Fundraiser

In his book *Lessons in Leadership*, the late Rabbi Lord Jonathan Sacks touches on *chillul Hashem* and *kiddush Hashem* (Hebrew for "desecrating and sanctifying God's name," respectively).

Rabbi Sacks states, "When we behave in such a way to evoke admiration for Judaism as a faith and a way of life that is a *kiddush Hashem*, a sanctification of God's name. When we do the opposite, when we betray that faith and way of life, causing people to have contempt for the God of Israel, that is a *chillul Hashem*."

Sacks retells the story of Mendel the waiter, originally told by the late Rabbi Norman Lamm, formerly the chancellor of Yeshiva University. When the daring rescue of Entebbe occurred in 1976, passengers on a cruise ship wanted to pay tribute to the Jewish people. The captain conducted a search and found only one crew member who was Jewish. He found Mendel, a waiter on the ship, and in a solemn ceremony offered congratulations on behalf of the crew and passengers to Mendel who became the de facto ambassador of the Jewish nation. All Jews become ambassadors of the Jewish people when how they live, behave and treat others become fodder for the public square.

Conversely, when Jews act badly, crooks like Bernie Madoff, Jewish sex offenders or Jewish celebrities, politicians or religious persons who act inappropriately, they desecrate God's name and taint the world's view of all Jews.

This issue is highly germane to our topic. Anyone involved in raising funds has an obligation to act ethically in his or her noble work. When representing a Jewish organization, or any organization for that matter, how one performs in public will dictate how Jews, the Jewish faith and how Hashem (God) are perceived by the world.

I am a member of the Association of Fundraising Professionals (AFP), the trade association representing thousands of professional fundraisers. We must adhere to the national code of ethics promulgated by the AFP. For example, code #21 states that professional fundraisers "...not accept compensation or enter into a contract that is based on a percentage of contributions; nor shall members accept finder's fees or contingent fees."

Unfortunately, there are nonprofits that do not follow this rule.

Charity Navigator objectively rates charitable organizations for trust and support. Inherent in the nonprofit's financial health, transparency and accountability is a principal mandate to meet ethical standards. On its website, Charity Navigator states, "Our ratings show givers how efficiently we believe a charity will use their support today, how well it has sustained its programs and services over time and their level of commitment to good governance, best practices and openness with information."

Good ethical conduct is, therefore, a condition in achieving Charity Navigator's mission. Objective professional evaluators of charities mirror the same approach.

I have compiled a short, albeit inexhaustible, list of ethical markers, some dos and don'ts, that fundraisers and organizations they represent should consider as part of an ethical fundraising approach.:

1) Commissions by fundraisers based on a percentage of what they raise are an inappropriate and unethical form of compensation. As a donor, I don't want to find out that a sizable chunk of my donation went to the fundraiser. Appropriate forms of compensation include salary, project allowances and even bonuses for high-level performance.

2) Do what you say you are going to do. Meet or exceed donor expectations, and set high standards.

3) Be honest in your endeavors including all communications with the public.

4) Always follow the rule of law, respect donor privacy and intent, as well as acknowledge donor gifts in a prompt fashion.

5) Run campaigns that are real and not "of-the-moment." Some organizations run specious campaigns contending these will establish a program or a building. Time elapses, and no program or buildings appear. "Of-the-moment" campaigns ruin credibility and future prospects for support.

6) Commemorative dedications are a sensitive topic. Some organizations remove plaques or naming gifts from buildings without seeking permission from the donors or families. Unless the donor did not fulfill the pledge, removing a commemoration is unethical and inappropriate.

7) Fundraising expenses should, at most, not exceed 35 percent of revenue collected. This yardstick assures that the majority of funds raised are used for their intended purpose. Obviously, the less spent on fundraising expense and the more distributed to services the better.

8) Don't spend money lavishly for transportation, personal amenities or expensive gifts or premiums for donors. It's simply unethical and wrong.

There are, of course, many more benchmarks we can cite. But these are minimum expectations. The National Council of Nonprofits says,

"Transparency inspires confidence. Beyond what the law requires, nonprofits can demonstrate their commitment to ethical practices by being entirely transparent with financial information and fundraising practices."

So, I ask you as an ethical fundraiser, or as an organization raising funds, are you interested in desecrating or sanctifying God's name?

CHAPTER THIRTY-THREE
To Institute a
Direct Mail Program
or Not?

Is your mailbox bombarded by nonprofits asking for your fundraising dollars? Your mailbox is overflowing, especially during the holidays. What you are getting is politely known in the vernacular as "junk mail." Yet, these mailbox assaults persist, and some feel is growing exponentially. If you are a nonprofit organization, and have not done direct mail solicitations to the masses, you must ask yourself, "Do I start a direct mail program or not?"

The simple answer for some is, "You've got to be in it to win it." Not so fast. This chapter may shake reality into those first considering this possibility.

Negev Direct Marketing is one of the largest direct mail providers to Jewish nonprofit organizations. In one of his blogs, Yoav Kaufman, a principal of this firm, presented an interesting fact that "92% of Millennials say they are more influenced by direct mail than any other form of marketing. Couple that with the fact that 81% of all consumers say they read or at least scan direct mail...." That's the good news.

Consider the following. There are many nonprofits in the United States that rely heavily on fundraising dollars generated by direct mail programs. These include, but are not limited to, the American Cancer Society, American Heart Association, March of Dimes, Easter Seals and the list goes on. These nonprofits have a long and successful record using direct mail. Studies show that many older donors look forward to these mailings and often feel as if each letter is personally addressed to them. This is not junk mail in their world. It is staying in touch with family, and they would miss the connection if the chain was broken.

I predict that, in time, the Millennial generation will change today's mail dynamic. Millennials compose approximately 20 percent of philanthropic donations today, while 80 percent of gifts stem from the Baby Boomer or older generations. Baby Boomers are used to seeing junk mail in their mailboxes. Let's talk again in ten to fifteen years, and I suspect things will have changed.

There are many pros and cons about starting a direct mail program. What is compelling is this reality: most start-up direct mail programs lose money. The national response rate for direct mail is grim. Responses generally range between 1 to 3 percent. Ouch! Those mean folks don't care about what you have to say and ignore your pleas for support? That's right. But if you want to look at the glass being half full, then consider that 1 to 3 percent heard you and responded affirmatively. Well, maybe, not half full.

You may have read that many major nonprofits make millions on their mailings. True. However, they have long and consistent histories with successful campaigns. They also have a finely hewn mail program that came about after years of tried and tested experience. A new start-up campaign is usually not so lucky. But I digress. Luck really has nothing to do with it.

What variables should a nonprofit consider? You may wish to talk to a direct mail expert. It is a specialized industry, and consultants are easily found in professional literature such as in *The Chronicle of Philanthropy*. Here are just some of the issues:

1) Volume—how many total units are you mailing?
2) How many pieces are you including in the mailing (e.g., a four-piece mailing, which includes a cover letter, mailing envelope, return or business reply envelope commonly known as a BRE and an insert such as a pledge card)?
3) What are the sizes of all pieces?
4) Is there a premium or giveaway included such as a calendar, mailing labels or a pen?
5) What will the postage fee be (first class or bulk mail)?
6) Mailing list—is it up to date?
7) Will you need rental lists?
8) Will you need a fulfillment house to process the mailing, or do you have a volunteer corps to do it?
9) Are you registered to conduct charitable solicitations in other states?

There are many other variables to consider, including when to mail, themes, complementary and simultaneous web campaigns to run, securing new donors or new acquisitions, retaining current donors and bringing back lapsed donors, and here is the most important one—*the message*. My goodness. The list is endless. Are you sure you want to do this?

A direct mail campaign requires nerves of steel, skill and a determination to succeed despite the odds.

Are you ready to invade your neighbor's mailbox?

122

CHAPTER THIRTY-FOUR
What is a Case Statement, and Do I Need One?

When I started my career in fundraising, the catchphrase question I heard most often was, "Where is your case statement?" This became very intimidating, because I had no idea what a case statement was and whether I needed one. After a while, I was determined to learn about it, and so, I did my due diligence.

The first time it came to my attention was when the nonprofit I worked for embarked on a capital campaign. We were planning a 120-bed addition to a Jewish Home for the Elderly, which would serve, in large part, a growing population of residents with dementia and Alzheimer's type of disease. The addition to an existing 120-bed institution was to be an ultramodern facility with a plethora of innovative design and construction features.

Our fundraising goal was to demographically canvass the county in which we were found, and meet with major philanthropists we knew lived there. The bulk of these affluent benefactors lived in six to seven major communities, and it required a concerted effort by our campaign leadership to arrange meetings in various venues including homes, country clubs, restaurants and business offices.

As part of our strategic fundraising plan, we created a case statement to present to prospective donors. So, what is it?

In brief, a case statement must live up to its name: it presents your case for support. It demonstrates identified community needs and, in a persuasive way, how you will address and solve those needs, why you are uniquely qualified to address these needs and what the benefits are that will accrue from your actions. The case statement can be used to launch campaigns or simply introduce your organization and solicit general support.

Case statements usually are brochures that come in all shapes and varieties. But most have some common denominators that appeal to the folks from whom you are soliciting funds.

A case statement brochure should be aesthetic looking. It should be attractive and invite a donor's attention. But it should not be ostentatious or overly lavish. Otherwise, the donor has every right to say that you are throwing away good money on a wasteful printing exercise. If you are appealing to high-net-worth individuals, then give the brochure a prominent appearance much like a corporate annual report. Size doesn't usually matter, but it should be large enough to be easily held, be straightforwardly engaging to the reader and, most important, be persuasive.

Remember, one picture is worth a thousand words. Whatever you promote should be captured with compelling photography that helps tell your story in a powerful way. If you promote bricks and mortar, then display new design features, model buildings and groundbreaking qualities. If it's not yet built, have the architect or interior designer share illustrations populated with colorful graphics, pioneering characteristics and people.

Brevity is always a positive attribute. We live in the age of sound bites. Each section should supply sufficient information to describe all aspects of your project or programs. Your narrative should be descriptive, but not an addendum to *War and Peace*. People's attention span is limited. Be concise. Keep to a minimum the information you need to convey to the prospect. There are many graphic features you can use, such as pull quotes, to get your point across. However, a discussion about these is outside the purview of this chapter.

So, what are some of the specifics to impart? Here is a short compilation of suggestions:

1) Theme and organizational logo
2) Mission statement
3) Lay and staff leadership
4) Facts and information about the nonprofit
5) Narrative describing the case for support
6) A case study or two
7) Commemorations and dedications
8) Ways to help the organization
9) Metrics, budgets and graphs

There are other essentials that you will consider such as contact and tax-exempt information, website and the like, but the above are some of the key elements you may want to incorporate. No two nonprofits are alike, and you must adapt your case statement to your specific needs.

So, what will it be, a case statement or an excuse statement?

STRATEGIC
FUNDRAISING
GROUP LLC

CHAPTER THIRTY-FIVE
When "No" Doesn't Mean No!

One of the challenges facing fundraisers in the nonprofit world, and for that matter anywhere, is rejection. No one likes being rebuffed, especially a professional fundraiser. But it's inevitable. Some studies show that only one in twenty solicitations is successful. Not a good batting average for a baseball player, but often bleak reality for those raising funds.

I have often found, however, that sometimes rejection is not what you think it is. It takes skill, intuition, ingenuity, understanding of human behavior and sometimes just dumb luck to read the signs. Sometimes the telltale signs are staring you in the face, but you must be perceptive enough to read them. Let's illustrate.

One donor I once visited greeted me with a non-customary grunt instead of his usual cordial greeting. We went back a long way, and it wasn't like him to be less than friendly. After some prodding, I learned that he hadn't experienced a good day, at the very least. His financial portfolio was tanking in the markets, he had a dispute with a business associate that day and he banged up his knee on his way in to work. That's enough to put a dour face on anyone. It was clear that his response to my solicitation for a favorite project wasn't going to yield a favorable result that day, so my Plan B sprang into action.

Instead of pushing for a gift that I felt, instinctively, would end in a "no," the meeting turned into a brief, but informative, progress report on the project. This was not the right time to ask for a major gift. There would be other opportunities. At the end of the conversation, the donor appreciated my sensitivity to his day of turmoil and thanked me for coming by *not* to solicit money, but to brief him on our progress and also seek his advice on a related matter. The meeting ended well, albeit with no donation.

When I returned to try again about six weeks later, he was in a cheery mood, and a generous gift was the result of our get-together. No confluence of bad news that day.

I use this story to make a point. There simply are times when it's best to back off and try another approach or visit at another time. "No" that day wasn't a definitive "no" forever, just that day. The seasoned professional, and the up-and-coming volunteer or lay leader, should learn to recognize when "no" doesn't mean no!

Mitigating circumstances can wreak havoc on a solicitor's dream. Keep these thoughts in mind when reaching out to your donor for a pledge or contribution.

Part of entering into a dialogue with a contributor is his or her frame of mind, body language and activities happening around him or her. Judge the mood. Is the donor friendly, happy, receptive and not distracted?

Keep in mind that circumstances beyond your control will affect your success that day. Did the donor have a spat with his or her spouse? Was there a business setback that day or recently? Did a family member or close friend come down with an illness? Did the dog eat the homework or chew up a favorite shoe? The list is endless. So here are some pointers to consider when facing possible rejection by a donor:

1) "No" may mean "not today or the present." Find out whether you might revisit the subject some other time.

2) "No" may mean "I am not interested in your project." This means it's time to recalibrate and come back another time with a different proposal.
3) "No" may mean that you are asking too much from this donor. Perhaps a more modest ask is in order.
4) "No" may mean that the donor wants to consult with his or her spouse and then will be able to respond. This happens frequently. Don't be put off.
5) "No" may mean that you're using the wrong approach for this project. Rethink what you are doing, saying and see if there is a better way to approach the donor.
6) "No" may mean you have bad personal chemistry with the donor. Perhaps another solicitor is necessary. What's more important, the gift or your ego?
7) "No" may mean absolutely "No way" and will require research to understand what's bothering your donor.

There may be a myriad of reasons why the donor declined your proposal. What is important is to discern whether "No" is a temporary setback or a permanent response.

The real question is this: are you prepared for rejection, and can you bounce back?

CHAPTER THIRTY-SIX
When Should You Cancel
(or Postpone) Your Special Event?
PART I

There comes a time in virtually every fundraiser's life when he or she is faced with a crisis that threatens staging the nonprofit's special event. At such times, the dilemma may revolve around cancelling or postponing a special event that may have been months, or even a year, in the planning.

For purposes of public disclosure, I never cancelled or postponed a major event, but came awfully close.

Let me state from the outset that I faced two such crises. Staying calm, cool and collected was what got me through both, but it's always easy to say so in retrospect. Serious heart palpitations, sleeplessness and profuse sweat under the brow were probably more what I experienced than I care to admit. Let's go back in time and relive these nightmares.

I worked for one organization for whom I ran the annual golf outing. Our tournaments were always sold out, and we generated significant revenue from these events. At first, we sold 144 player slots that encompassed an entire golf course. Subsequently, the tournament became so wildly popular that we had to use two golf courses to accommodate the many players that signed up. It was a great fundraiser, as well as a wonderful public relations and marketing tool.

These events usually occurred on a Monday since most of the country clubs consider it an off day when their membership does not golf on their course, which opens up the club to nonprofits and others who rent the course for the day. As a sidebar, no one ever went hungry at these golf events, because the day started with a lavish breakfast, followed by sumptuous barbeques on the course at converging holes. After the players completed play, they repasted over an exquisite cocktail hour with pass-arounds, carving stations and hot chafing dishes. All of this ended with a grand awards banquet that featured the finest steaks and gourmet dishes. Hungry you were not.

The golf event I ran on this occasion was held at a beautiful club in Westchester County. I remember driving on the Merritt Parkway at 7:00 A.M. that day looking out at a blue sky and a radiant sun. What occurred the preceding week is what rocked my world that morning. The club manager called me and asked the following question: "Norm, would you mind if we postponed the golf tournament until next Monday?"

I was thinking, *Oh my God, oh my God, oh my God!*

Instead, I responded politely, "What seems to be the problem?"

The manager then informed me: "Well, Norm, as you know, we have had serious rain during the past week and the seventh hole, among others, is under water. Our drainage system is overwhelmed. My groundskeeper tells me that no one can play under these conditions."

I was thinking, *Oh my God, oh my God, oh my God!*

Instead, I responded calmly, "Frank, I am only a few minutes away. Why don't we assess the situation when I get there?" He reluctantly agreed, but also said it was unlikely play would take place.

I was thinking, *Oh my God, oh my God, oh my God!*

I immediately contacted the executive vice president and president of my organization. The club manager contacted his board president, as well. Time was short, and a decision had to be made quickly. Keep in mind that we had folks flying in from out of state, as well as others traveling from Long Island, Brooklyn and other parts unknown and there was *no way* they, or their guests, could be contacted in time. Did I tell you about the heart palpitations?

As long as safety was assured, my executive VP and board president did not want to cancel or postpone the event, which was months in the planning. Their board president was reluctant to approve moving forward. When I arrived, we met with the groundskeeper, manager and arranged for all the other parties to join on a tense conference call.

To make a long story short, we agreed to a compromise. Instead of using golf carts around the course, all players had to walk the course except for anyone with a heart condition, physical challenges or the like. They could use carts on the concrete covered areas, but nowhere else. Well, at least everyone got their exercise on that sweltering summer day.

Space limits my telling you in this chapter about the second crisis. You need to read on.

In the next chapter, I also will offer some practical solutions. Stay tuned.

CHAPTER THIRTY-SEVEN
When Should You Cancel
(or Postpone) Your Special Event?
PART II

When we left the last chapter's cliffhanger, I explained how close I came to cancelling or, at a minimum, postponing a major golf tournament. Thanks to nerves of steel and help from the One Above, many months of planning were not wasted, and we had an eminently successful event that made lots of money.

On to the next Fear Factor episode.

I was the executive producer of both the Jewish Hospice and OHEL Benefit Concerts in New York. One year, we booked the Marquis Theatre on Broadway and featured a stellar concert cast. Our goal always was to create firsts—unique concerts with innovations never done before—to give each event its own brand of excitement. One year, not only were we inaugurating a popular Jewish Chassidic concert on Broadway, we were planning to dedicate a Torah scroll, something also never carried out before on Broadway.

One month before the concert, rumblings of a stagehands strike at *all* Broadway theatres surfaced in the news. We were nervous, but nothing definitive was announced so we hoped for the best. A week before the event, our worst fears came to pass, and the stagehands struck and picketers amid wooden horses surrounded *our* theatre and all others on Broadway day and night.

Thousands of tickets had been sold, the theatre had been paid its hefty non-refundable deposit, and other expenses had been paid in advance such as catering, promotional materials, performer down payments and equipment rentals.

A decision had to be made. Keep in mind that our theatre rental was only good for that one night, and any postponement would have been difficult since no other dates were available to us at the Marquis Theatre. What to do?

Our concert committee agreed on a deadline. If we could not resolve the situation by 5:00 P.M. the day before the concert date, we would hit the airwaves with cancellation notices. Ticket and sponsor refunds would be made, and months of planning would evaporate.

An unlikely hero came to the rescue. There was a New York City public advocate at the time who was very connected with the stagehands' union. He was a good friend, and he went to bat for us. I was regularly in touch with him and he kept me apprised of the situation. He knew we had a deadline, 5:00 P.M. the day before, so he conducted serious negotiations with the union on our behalf throughout the night and following day.

It looked grim. At 4:55 P.M., I received a call from the public advocate who informed me that he had negotiated a cessation of the picketing for the one day of our concert and we could carry on. All the picket signs, wooden horses and protesters would be gone, and the concert would go on as scheduled. That unlikely hero was none other than *Bill DeBlasio*, who would someday become the mayor of New York! Our concert was a major success.

So, what are the lessons to be learned from these two major events that were almost cancelled? There are some critical steps a nonprofit should consider and/or take when planning a major event, whether indoors or outdoors, and these include the following:

1) Cancellation insurance is necessary when preparing for a major event. In our cases, a significant amount of money could have been forfeited. I have seen monsoon type of rains that caused some golf tournaments to be cancelled or at least postponed. Cancellation insurance should cover both expected revenue and expenses, and avert a financial catastrophe.

2) Follow the "Pikuach Nefesh" (Hebrew for "a life put in danger") doctrine. There are times when inclement weather simply requires a cancellation or, at a minimum, a postponement. Don't risk safety and security—ever! Today, there are events where participants rappel off a thirty-story building, take part in crazy marathons or become involved in an event where other acts of God can seriously mar the happening. Highly publicized events also can draw unsavory characters who can severely affect the nonprofit's fundraiser. Prepare for extenuating circumstances.

3) *Always* formulate a contingency plan. Every case is different, so I cannot offer a specific response to every situation. This is for your committee to discuss.

4) Remember that how you cancel or postpone a major event may affect your organization's reputation. Be sure to give special consideration as to how you offer ticket and sponsor refunds. It may dictate your financial success or failure next time.

5) Communicate your decision *quickly* to everyone at least twenty-four hours before the event. Use all viable means of communication.

6) Be sure to have a committee whom you can trust to make the right decision. This is not a decision for just one person. The president, chair of the board, committee chair and/or senior executive should be invested with the ultimate decision making.

7) Finally, we live in a crazy world. Safety and security must be paramount in your mind. Make sure to take the necessary precautions.

Is your nonprofit ready to raise some significant funds from your major event? Good. Then also be prepared to save a lot of money in case you face the adversity of a disastrous cancellation or postponement.

Are you all set?

STRATEGIC
FUNDRAISING
GROUP LLC

CHAPTER THIRTY-EIGHT
When Things Go Wrong
PART I

Life is not fair (where have you heard that before?). Would you like another insightful saying? How about "Mensch tracht, uhn Gott lacht"? The loose translation from the Yiddish is, "A person thinks, and God laughs." We know that people make plans, and then life happens. I went through some personal angst not long ago because a general contractor reneged on his contract. Things couldn't go more wrong. It was a painful experience, but I got through it.

But what happens when you plan a fundraiser for hundreds of people and things go wrong? What do you do? My best advice is to think fast on your feet. There usually isn't a set script to follow. One must improvise and invent. A mentor of mine once declared, "When you put your inventor's cap on, you are only limited by your creativity." This means that you have unlimited potential to solve problems. So, put on your inventor's cap when things go wrong.

I was fortunate during my professional career to have few things go wrong. But it happened and, fortunately, I was able to think quickly on my feet, as were some of my esteemed colleagues who worked alongside me. We produced good solutions to vexing problems that could have been far more serious. Let me give you an example.

Anyone who knows me well realizes that I am not a fan of fundraising journals (read the chapter entitled "Do Fundraising Journals Make Attractive Doorstops?"). Fortunately, more and more nonprofits are seeing the light and have begun to phase out these doorstops for more creative options such as scrolls of honor, flash drives with donor commemorations and sometimes just rolling audio-visual credits on a large screen at a major event.

However, when journals were still singularly in vogue, I created one that was unique—an executive desk planner. It was calendared by week, and folks could mark in their daily appointments. Today this approach is totally obsolete since we carry calendars on our mobile devices. At that time, devices such as Palm Pilots were in their inception phase and among the prehistoric creatures starting an electronic trend.

As a cost-saving measure, a colleague convinced me to use a new printer who could shave off substantial dollars from the cost of printing the journal, which can be an expensive endeavor. The journal was to be distributed at our annual dinner, which that year took place in Manhattan at The Plaza Hotel then owned by Donald and Ivana Trump. We expected six hundred or more distinguished guests in the main ballroom, and the room was beautifully appointed and ready. Both Donald and Ivana visited just prior to the event and complimented us on how attractively we had decorated the hall.

I remained at The Plaza all day, and as we got closer to the start time of the gala, 6:00 P.M., I kept looking at my watch, yet no journals had arrived. 3:00 P.M., no journals. 4:00 P.M., no journals. 4:30 P.M., no journals. My heart was pumping faster, and the printer was not returning my urgent calls. It was 5:00 P.M. and still no journals! Finally, at 5:20 P.M., boxes showed up at the ballroom door. I began to feel much better.

And then . . . I opened the boxes and, to my mortification, found that many journal pages were smeared inside because the ink hadn't yet dried. On top of that—we'd decided that all pages should be inserted into an elegant loose-leaf binder so that the binder remained, but the calendar pages could be replaced every year—many journals had pages inserted upside down. Good grief! What to do?

We quickly assembled our staff and volunteers, and did a quick assessment. Half of the journals were dry, but had to have their pages turned right side up. We set up an assembly line and by 6:00 P.M. distributed all the journals we could use. No guests complained, and enough were spread around the room. Disaster averted.

In Part II of this series, I will describe some ingenious solutions to other projects that went wrong. If it happens to you, just don't panic; keep a calm demeanor and remember to put on your inventor's cap. To paraphrase from the poem by Robert Burns, just know that the best laid plans of mice and men so often go astray.

STRATEGIC FUNDRAISING GROUP LLC

CHAPTER THIRTY-NINE
When Things Go Wrong
PART II

If you follow my essays, you know that I firmly believe in the dictum "Proper prior planning prevents poor performance" (see chapter called "Are Rules of Thumb for the Dumb?"). And yet, we know that, even with meticulous planning, things sometimes go awry because we are not always in charge of our destinies. Last chapter I referred to one such instance and how I improvised to remedy, what would have been, a seriously embarrassing problem with a fundraising journal.

A setback with an impending fundraiser usually can be predicted because of past experiences. At other times, things can go wrong during the event itself, and you need to be primed and ready. Let me give you an example of each instance and how these were handled.

The first case occurred when I planned a bike-a-thon for a nonprofit. More nonprofits have added bike rides to their arsenal of fundraising options for various reasons. Bike riding is a popular form of fundraising for nonprofits because it is an upbeat event, it promotes healthy living and, among other things, it is a trendy social happening. What brings in large sums of money are lucrative sponsorships.

Seemed like a no-brainer. So, we formed a committee of bike enthusiasts who we felt would help us plan and recruit many other cyclists. Instead, they preoccupied themselves with the minutiae of the event.

Their main concerns revolved around the bike route, rest stations, refreshments, support wagons, EMT support, swag bags, biker bibs, insurance, permits, police involvement and a myriad of other resources needed. All of these, and more, are critical logistical details that obviously must be addressed. However, what they did not spend time doing—and what we needed from them the most—was *fundraising*.

We went this route for several years and raised some money. But the time and resources expended were disproportionately greater than the funds brought in. It wasn't worth it. So, what was the solution?

The answer was simple. There are existing bike tours you can buy into and still raise big funds. For example, in New York, there is the annual TD Bank Five Borough Bike Tour in which more than thirty-two thousand cyclists take part. TD Bank plans all the logistics. If you get in early enough, the nonprofit can have a healthy contingent of bike riders and raise a sizeable sum. We joined the TD Tour and raised a significant amount of money. And we did not, unnecessarily, consume time and resources.

Then there is the example of a problem with a fundraiser that occurred on the spot and needed immediate attention.

I was the executive producer of a major annual concert series that held most of its events at Lincoln Center in New York. One year, we initiated a new and unique concert idea. Instead of just musical performances, we created a script with a storyline and melded filmed scenes with live performances onstage. It was a unique concept that also incorporated into each scene merchant advertising that brought in a brand-new revenue stream.

The show required our performers to act and memorize lines, in addition to their musical performances. It was an exciting show, and the nonprofit sold out well in advance of the concert. All went well, except with one high-level performer. He couldn't memorize his lines. He assured us that, when we got to the concert, he would be fine. The day of the concert arrived, and despite plentiful rehearsals, he stumbled over his lines. What to do?

It required an ingenious solution. We quickly secured high-tech communications equipment like the kind you see used by the Secret Service or as seen on TV action-drama shows. The performer was supplied with a micro-sized earbud communication device invisible on the stage. During his performance, our scriptwriter literally read him his lines from the projection booth, and he simply repeated them with the right emphasis. No one was the wiser, and the event was a huge success.

The two examples I described were predicated on different situations. The first was based on painful experience. We learned from our mistakes. The second was founded on a more urgent situation that needed an instantaneous resolution. Improvisation lent itself to our success.

Now, what would you do in each case?

STRATEGIC
FUNDRAISING
GROUP LLC

CHAPTER FORTY
Yes, Fundraising is a Team Sport

Fundraisers and elite Navy SEALs have much in common. Both are highly dependent on synchronization with others on their teams. In the military, teamwork is *essential*, as the life of one soldier is dependent on the actions of others in his/her unit. On a much lesser scale of danger, seasoned fundraisers know that individual success is often contingent on the actions of fellow staff.

I have for a long time adhered to former NY Yankee manager Joe Torre's philosophy that there is no "I" in "team." It's true in baseball, and it's true in fundraising. And yet there is the epic story told of Michael Jordan, the great Chicago Bulls basketball Hall of Famer, who in the fever pitch close of a tied playoff game was reminded of this dictum by his coach who wanted to give the final shot to another player. Michael snapped, "Yes, but there is an 'I' in 'win.' Give me the dang ball, coach!"

So, when do the needs of the few or even one outweigh the needs of the many, and when do the needs of the many outweigh the needs of the individual or the few? No, this column is not about *Star Trek*, nor is it about opposing teams organized to compete against each other. It's about how fundraising requires staff and volunteers to work together as one unit to achieve a common goal.

Having been part of assorted development efforts, I will personally vouch for the necessity to have an all-hands-on-deck approach with most fundraising activities. Let me express profound appreciation to my colleagues and lay leaders who worked with me and collaborated on many a project on behalf of our nonprofits. We raised a lot of money, and it was primarily because we planned and worked together as a cohesive group and not as individuals.

There are many building blocks in an initiative-taking and dynamic fundraising program. These include, but are not limited to, major gifts, special events, direct mail solicitations, web campaigns and many grassroots efforts. Whether you are in a small shop as a full-time, or as a part-time, fundraiser, one usually depends on the goodwill, skills and involvement of others to be successful. You are generally dependent upon board leadership, volunteers and friends of the organization. There is no circumventing this fact.

For those in the throes of a special event such as an annual dinner, it becomes clear to everyone that the team, in the words of an old cliché, represents many cogs in a wheel that make it go around. If one of the cogs malfunctions, it affects the sturdiness of that round wheel and can mean the difference between success and failure. All cogs in the wheel must be in sync to assure an effective result.

To carry this notion further, let's look at some of the many elements necessary when coordinating a special event, such as an annual dinner, that best exemplify team effort. Here is a small checklist, each of which requires its own team configuration:

1) Invitations (hard copy and/or evite plus mailing)
2) Event site acquisition and coordination
3) Catering and menu
4) Program and schedule
5) Entertainment (when appropriate)
6) Registration
7) Seating arrangements

8) Advertising and publicity

9) Audio-visual requirements

10) Volunteers such as greeters and facilitators

This preliminary checklist is easily expanded, because every special event is unique and brings its own issues and logistical considerations. But you get the idea.

I have been privileged to run annual and capital campaigns, as well as planned giving and endowment fund programs. These efforts require the professional fundraiser to mobilize collegial and/or lay leader support to initiate or implement these undertakings. One must be grateful to all the folks that help and participate, because without their valued collaboration, the programs go nowhere.

Occasionally, I am asked whether face-to-face philanthropy or 1:1 solicitations requires team participation. After all, when one approaches a donor, it's only you and the prospect, right? Truth be told, there usually is a team behind such efforts. In some instances, a researcher collects and provides background information on the prospect. There may be friends, family or business associates that offer advice about how best to solicit the donor. Colleagues may be consulted, and after the meeting, a gift may need to be recorded. The point is there are others behind the scenes that play a vital role. They may just be invisible to the naked eye. But we are grateful they are behind the ubiquitous curtain.

There is a wise saying: "Talent wins games, but teamwork and intelligence win championships." When a major donor makes a significant gift and joins your team, it feels like having won a championship.

So, are you ready to be a team player, or do you indulge in individual sports?

CHAPTER FORTY-ONE
Is Fundraising a Solo Act?

For ten years, I was privileged to work with the late great public relations impresario Howard Rubenstein (see my reference to Howard Rubenstein in the "Introduction"). The organization I worked for was growing exponentially, and by the time I left, it was a $750 million-a-year enterprise. An organization that size required a smart and consistent public relations campaign, and I was the fortunate beneficent who learned from the master and the account executives he assigned to me.

Howard Rubenstein was a master of the PR trade and a strategic thinker. His firm represented major corporations and the elite in the business and political world. Watching him in action was an edifying experience, one I won't forget. He was adept at handling highly delicate and often volatile people and situations. His clients ranged from Donald Trump, the New York Yankees ownership and Rupert Murdoch, to major celebrities and political figures. His forte was good PR and, when necessary, damage control.

While Rubenstein wasn't a fundraiser per se, he understood the indispensable and symbiotic nature of public relations and development. He understood that a well-placed story in the *New York Times* or *Wall Street Journal* can yield epic philanthropic gifts, and not necessarily from donors in the immediate service area, because the media's geographic span is far reaching.

Rubenstein once showed me a front-page story he placed in the *Wall Street Journal* about a nonprofit that fought to protect endangered species. One of the programs they featured was a conservation program that safeguarded ecological communities. It turned out that a wealthy animal lover in Alaska read the article and was so enthralled he mailed a $1 million check to the organization! An important lesson learned was that we simply don't know what touches someone, even if that person is way across the country. Pitching stories that the media publish or showcase is an important means to sway philanthropists interested in your cause. Maintaining an initiative-taking public relations campaign is integral to your fundraising efforts.

The synergy of a well-defined marketing program in tandem with a strategic fundraising program also is an effective way of catching the eye of contributors. A chief focus of marketing includes branding and advertising that imprint critical messages you want donors to hang on to about your institution. The central theme of one of our branding campaigns was "honoring our parents," a biblical imperative that resonated with our community. It was honest and helped propel our $16 million capital campaign to a triumphant conclusion.

So, what are the tools in today's high-tech era that will project your message to constituents? Never have we been blessed with such an arsenal of firepower to succeed in our quest to raise money for any charity. But first, you must define your PR and marketing goals. And whether you are a new nonprofit or one that has been around for decades makes no difference. Don't assume your constituents know everything there is to know about you. And yes, that goes even more so for your board of directors.

Oh. Did I say something politically indelicate?

Your goals are straightforward. They are as follows:

1) Create a message that resonates with your constituency.
2) Establish strategic plans for your fundraising, PR and marketing campaigns, and be sure to link them.
3) Inform the community you serve about your programs and services to attract interest in them.
4) Communicate positive reviews and charity watchdog rankings that place you above the competition.
5) Cast your institution in a positive light with your successes.
6) Differentiate yourself from the competitors.
7) Stimulate fund giving with a variety of giving opportunities.
8) Share how you mobilized community support on your behalf.
9) Instill brand name recognition in the communities you serve.
10) Secure feedback from your board and/or lay leadership.

We live in a digital age when you are only limited by your creativity in getting the word out. Use websites, social media, e-newsletters, e-blasts and other online or digital initiatives to bring your organization to the forefront because, remember, you have plenty of competition. And always resort to conventional means to spread the word, such as annual reports, press releases, direct mail appeals, hard copy newsletters and the like. Just keep your inventor's hat on, and keep inventing.

Howard Rubenstein was described as a "master of relationships and making connections." But as imaginative as he was, he was not a solo act. He relied on many resources to make his name.

When raising funds, can you claim the same?

STRATEGIC
FUNDRAISING
GROUP LLC

CHAPTER FORTY-TWO
Raising Funds for the Incarcerated

There are a select few who regularly visit Jewish prisoners held in federal, state or even local prisons. But there is a necessity for this service, and like most nonprofit endeavors, it requires financial support no different than programs set up to serve individuals with specialized needs. They may require kosher meals, prayer books, prayer shawls, Bibles and other Jewish artifacts to properly observe Sabbath or major Jewish holiday rituals.

Undoubtedly, raising funds to enhance the lives of the incarcerated is a huge challenge. Depending on whether it is for a white- or blue-collar crime, some folks believe that their imprisonment is well-deserved punishment. Their line of thinking, whether right or wrong, is that they are not entitled to special services. "Let them rot!" is an extreme opinion held by some who may not have given much thought to this issue.

And yet, the other more orthodox line of thinking is that these folks are serving a sentence meted out proportionate with their offense to society and, as such, are chastened enough. Their thinking is that incarceration with the right services is a form of rehabilitation so that, in many cases, inmates who complete their sentences can return and reintegrate into society having served out their prison term.

Whatever your thinking about such individuals, the reality is that there are many such offenders in jails across the country and, in my opinion, the humane approach is to offer them services so that they can celebrate Jewish customs or traditions no different than their fellow Christian or Muslim inmates.

I once had opportunity to visit Jewish prisoners in a federal detention center. While I had no heads-up descriptive profile of these inmates, I felt compelled to reach out to these individuals and let them know they weren't forgotten regardless of their dismal circumstances. It was also an opportunity to see whether I could summon up enough empathy that would serve as inspiration to raise donations to lighten their plight.

The building which housed the federal prison looked like most; the windows facing out were in the form of narrow slats. Very little sunlight penetrated these foreboding walls. The main lobby was like most any in office buildings, except that when you walked inside you faced a protective glass-enclosed reception area consisting of thick impact windowpanes behind which guards were posted to greet visitors.

There was paperwork to be completed and submitted in advance to the authorities before entering, and there was a designated coordinator in the prison who handled these requests. He greeted me during my visit to be sure everything went as arranged. When I arrived, the guard behind the glass asked me to complete more paperwork. It also required that I write down with whom I was meeting and their prisoner identification number. This information must match the forms sent in advance of the visit.

I ended up seeing three prisoners even though I was scheduled to meet with four. One man was transferred elsewhere in the interim between my visitor application and arrival at the detention center. Some folks were incarcerated there for only a short period of time until the authorities decided where they would spend the rest of their sentence.

Once my paperwork was completed, including giving the guard my personal identification (driver's license), I was requested to empty my pockets and put any loose belongings into a locker visible to the guards. Even the iron padlock for the locker was forbidding. It was a very thick lock with an attached steel chain. One could take the key inside, but that was about it.

Once all of this was done, I entered a side door near the reception area where another guard asked me to go through a TSA-like contraption where I held up my arms as you would in the security area at an airport. Of course, I had to go back and forth several times because the alarm buzzed until we discovered that the bobby pins holding my kippah (Hebrew for "skull cap") in place were the reason for the alarm.

After going through, I signed a visitors' log with the names of the prisoners I was scheduled to meet. The guard next stamped the top of my right hand as they do in an amusement park in case you want to return after taking a break. In the event of an emergency, it also signified that I was on a visit to the inmates. He then checked my hand with an ultraviolet light to confirm that the stamp worked. Next, I was ushered into a holding area for what felt like an interminable wait.

The surroundings resembled any office reception area, except for the drab grey walls and doors nearby that had steel-encased buttons requiring a guard to buzz you in. There was a decorated Christmas tree near my seating area marking the time of year. No Chanukah menorah was on display even though it also would have been proper for the time of year.

Finally, a guard came by to take me to the prisoners I was visiting. We went through a short hallway that brought us into the visitors' room. This area looked like a large lunchroom with bolted-down tables and swivel seating. As I entered, I faced a tall reception desk where guards were posted. Opposite the desk were four rows of swivel seats where prisoners waited patiently to greet their visitors. Behind the seating area were office-like rooms where private meetings took place behind glass-encased doors. These were used by attorneys representing their clients, or probation officers, among others visiting.

At the desk, I surrendered my paperwork to the guard and then faced the inmates and loudly called out the name of the prisoner I was visiting. In my case, the first prisoner I met with was a thirty-seven-year-old woman by the name of Judith (not real name or age) who was happy to see me. But I couldn't help but notice the crestfallen look of one inmate who was just informed that his visitor had cancelled.

I should point out that I did not ask for, nor did I seek out, information about their crimes. That's none of my business and is frankly their private matter. My purpose in being there was to bring some cheer, words of encouragement and some inspiration to these folks. That was what I set out to do.

Judith was a very polite and seemingly modest woman. She expressed thanks that I cared enough to make the two-hour trip to visit. She was exceptionally appreciative, especially since no one visited her regularly while she served an eighteen-month sentence of which she had already served six to seven months. She did not want her parents to visit because it would further distress them to see their daughter in this setting.

She said that the living conditions in this prison were stark and austere, and she admitted that it was difficult for her. Prior to being transferred here, she had been in another prison system where conditions, she said, were much better. But visits of this sort strengthened her faith, and she was surprisingly upbeat and positive when we met.

We talked about her background, and she told me that she immigrated with her family to America thirty years ago from Russia. Yet, she spoke excellent English without the trace of an accent. She also was deeply grateful to the local rabbi who came every week with grape juice and challah who made kiddush (blessing over the wine) and hamotzi (blessing over the challah) with her. She also was able to light candles for Chanukah using an electric menorah. She looked forward to serving out her sentence, re-entering society and becoming a worthy member of her community.

I next met with a young man in his twenties whom we will call Jeffrey. He stemmed from Florida and was from a seemingly middle-class family with whom he had lived before his imprisonment. Again, I was struck by his cheerful outlook and optimistic tone. He was on a floor where they had a minyan (a quorum for religious services). This was the group with which he spent time together during his stay and was currently several months into a six-month sentence.

He asked me if I could get him a pair of tzitzit (a four-corner fringed religious garment) to wear. He also was concerned about some fellow prisoners who each wanted a pair of tefillin (phylacteries). A siddur (prayer book) that he used was difficult for him to follow, and he asked if I could replace it with another that used a transliterated format. Hardly worries that I felt should be uppermost in his mind, and yet these were his major concerns. Once he finished his sentence, he felt that he would find an apartment, be on his own and not get into any more trouble. He was effusive in his thanks for my visit and for not forgetting him.

The last prisoner I met was a middle-aged man wearing a black crocheted kippah and a trimmed black beard. Let's call him Moshe. What blew me away was the story he told me. When he started serving his prison sentence, he was given a Tanach (Hebrew Bible). When he opened it up, it happened to open to Megillat Esther (the Purim story). The first thing that struck him was a sentence in Megillat Esther that told him right away that he was there for a reason—he felt that God thrust him into his situation for a reason—and with God's help and faith in the One Above, he would overcome his current circumstances. The sentence in the Megillah that astounded him occurs right after when

Haman's evil decree is overturned and the Jews of Shushan are given opportunity to defend themselves: "The Jews had light and gladness, and joy and honor." He firmly believed that this message was God sent and he would prevail despite his forty-six-month imprisonment.

He also told me that he was learning three *mesechtas* (tractates) of the Talmud while in jail. He was strong in his faith and Jewish observances and wanted to improve himself as much as possible. He described his three young children who were waiting for him on the outside and knew that one day he will rejoin his family and again become a productive member of society. He was confident and strong in his beliefs, which motivated him to endure what were, undeniably, uniquely challenging conditions. He too was profoundly grateful for my visit.

I wondered what words of encouragement I could offer each of the prisoners with whom I met, and it suddenly came to me from the portions of the Torah we read that month. The story of Joseph and his brothers came to mind. It is a story of "Surviving Failure" as the late Rabbi Lord Jonathan Sacks puts it in his book *Lessons in Leadership*. Joseph was thrown into a pit by his brothers. Then he was sold into slavery and taken to Egypt where, after the seduction episode with his master's wife, he was thrown into jail and stayed there until the pharaoh summoned him to interpret his dreams. Ultimately, he became the viceroy of Egypt second in command only to the pharaoh. When his brothers arrived, he and they achieved a sense of unity and reunification despite the harsh circumstances that got them there.

Each inmate, in his or her own way, felt they had survived failure. If there was one overriding message of positivity that I could leave with these prisoners, it was how Joseph and his brothers overcame and survived with a hopeful outcome. Each of the folks I met were grateful for this message of hope.

I left the prison that day and walked out into the bright sunlight knowing that in some small way I was able to bring a smidgeon of sunshine into their lives. I hope to return on other occasions and be further inspired by inmates who, because of their regrettable actions, are imprisoned. The visit reinforced my sincere belief that these stories would help me and any compassionate fundraiser, one with genuine empathy, to raise needed funds to help these lost souls.

Visiting the incarcerated is a great mitzvah (good deed), and it will bring a message of hope to those who need it. Try it. You'll like it.

CHAPTER FORTY-THREE
Is a Chinese Auction Worth It?

The advantage of writing a column is that my personal bias sometimes rises to the surface much like a water buoy bobbing up and down at sea. And like an oil slick, my partialities float on the surface for everyone to see. I am not a fan of Chinese auctions, but it is commonly used by nonprofits to raise major dollars and, for some, very successfully.

The origin of the term "Chinese auction" is unknown. In today's PC (politically correct) culture, it is sometimes just referred to as a penny sale. Some aficionados claim that it was meant to be called a "chance" auction because of the risky nature of the event—it *is* a game of chance. Somehow the appellation "Chinese" stuck, perhaps suggesting a secretive or mysterious type of event, making it more alluring.

Let's define what a Chinese auction is.

It's a nonprofit's fundraiser in which a combination of raffles and auctions are used to raise money from donated goods and services to the not-for-profit. These events primarily occur one of three ways: online on a website or in the virtual world, or from a catalogue sent to prospective donors via direct mail with instructions on how to participate, or at a live venue that also may feature entertainment, food, beverages and attractive displays showing the available goods and services.

The auction items usually have jars, baskets or boxes with slot openings placed in front of them to hold participant tickets. The more tickets you put into these containers, the greater the chances your ticket is pulled, and you win the item for which you are competing. The nonprofit needs to generate sales of as many tickets as possible to do well, sometimes including an admission fee.

Another way for the nonprofit to make money is to set up different price denominations for the tickets. For example, purchasing a ticket for a 65" Samsung large screen TV prize worth $600 is different than for a $50 Amazon gift card. If you want the classier prizes, you need to buy more expensive tickets for those containers.

Another popular format requires participants to place their tickets into one central basket where tickets can win any prize. In another format, each prize is auctioned off. Some Chinese auctions use all three formats to make the activity more fun and give it a feeling of variety. Some organizations add a 50:50 "split the pot" as another way to entice added ticket sales.

Here is why I am not a fan of this type of fundraiser. It is a labor-intensive project, and the return on investment (ROI) is not guaranteed. The ROI is usually a function of the quantity and quality of the prizes auctioned off. For example, if you have exclusive or luxurious prizes such as a fully appointed Lexus, diamond jewelry, fully paid cruises, major electronic equipment and the like, it will spur better sales. However, if your prizes are mediocre, don't expect a financial success.

Securing a sizable quantity of quality prizes requires a proactive committee with lots of volunteers, many of whom are themselves wealthy philanthropists who have the clout to secure well-appointed prizes and draw generous friends willing to lavish money on tickets. Presumably, the prizes are donated because having to spend money on expensive prizes is self-defeating. Having scores of volunteers to promote the Chinese auction before and during the event also is critical to its success.

Gambling worldwide is a very lucrative business. To an extent, Chinese auctions are a form of gambling. The gambling industry estimates that casino and online gambling alone is a $227-billion annual enterprise. Casinos, sports betting, fantasy sports are just some ways people indulge.

CNN Business reported that Americans spend billions of dollars each year on different games of chance. Close to $100 billion alone are raised in state-run lotteries such as the Powerball, electronic lottery games and traditional lottery or scratch off tickets. Regulars cannot get enough of games of chance, and this is why some of the big lotteries generate prizes close to $1 billion! And while most Americans don't play, it is estimated that adults in the United States spend an average of $325 on lottery tickets.

Gauging by the success of casino nights, poker events and raffles, a Chinese auction may be worth your while. But is it worth it? Unless you have the resources to pull it off, or a track record of success, don't bet on it.

CHAPTER FORTY-FOUR
Putting the Fun Back into *Fun*draising

There are nonprofits that get it, and there are those that don't.

While it isn't a well-publicized problem, I find that donors today suffer from battle fatigue. They are weary of relentless solicitations for their fundraising dollars. On several WhatsApp chat groups I joined, one well-known worthy cause asked for donations for several weeks straight *at least three times daily*! I call this the "sledgehammer" approach to fundraising, and it is a real turnoff.

Contributors to charities are regularly hit up from different directions, through personal solicitations, event-driven fundraisers, direct mail, online goings-on, synagogue/school/federation related occasions and even folks knocking on the door asking for "gelt" (Yiddish for "money"). After a while it takes its toll, and some philanthropists say "genook!" (Yiddish for "enough"). They may give less or even put a moratorium on giving—you just don't realize it.

I once had solicitors visit my home on a regular basis. It gave me pleasure to pull out the checkbook in front of my children to impress upon them the importance of charitable giving, *tzedakah*. But then word spread, and occasional such visitors suddenly became a torrent of schnorrers (Yiddish for "beggars"), and it was no longer a normal situation nor was it fun.

One day a solicitor came by and I wrote him a check. The size of the gift didn't please him, and he made an unflattering remark. He then gave me a cold stare and attitude. Another time I had a visitor ask me this disturbing question: "Can you tell me where all the Jews live?" Yet another caller told me he went from house to house in town just looking for the mezuzahs.

I lived in New Jersey then, and the local rabbinical council eventually adopted a vetting procedure for these solicitors, which included applying for a certificate attesting to the validity of their cause, as well as producing a laminated photo identification to prove they were who they claimed they were.

But I digress.

Yes, of course, philanthropists continue to give donations and will do so long into the future; I daresay for all eternity. They give for innumerable reasons, all of which aren't necessary to discuss here (see the chapter entitled "Why Do People Give?"). Suffice it to say that most people give because it's the moral thing to do, and the needs of those who need our support are great.

That doesn't mean that everyone enjoys giving donations the way they once did. So, my philosophy also has evolved. My current view is that it is important to put back the fun into *fun*draising. Not everyone agrees, but I believe fundraising without fun is like a circus without clowns or a sushi bar without a California roll. You get it!

It isn't always easy raising funds for a cause, especially sad ones. So, introducing a sense of joy or happiness with the charitable gift can be helpful. When I raised funds for terminally ill patients and their families, the challenge was bringing to a sad subject a sense of joyfulness that also lifted people's spirits. Despondent donors aren't good for business. If you transform melancholy supporters into happy ones, you will get repeat customers. For this reason, I created Hospice Celebrates Broadway as a way of putting *fun* back into fundraising and at the same time raising morale among families, patients and devotees of the hospice program.

Here is how it worked. At a pre-event food reception, we honored three distinguished personages such as successful local business entrepreneurs, admired philanthropists and influential community leaders. From the food venue, we went to a pre-selected Broadway show accompanied by upwards of six hundred patrons. The event had fun written all over it, and every year an increased number of sponsors joined us as the event gained popularity.

These activities also raised awareness for the program. At one home reception, we brought in a mentalist, at another venue we featured an unplugged acoustical event with Matisyahu (a reggae/alternate rock/hip hop artist) and in a third we introduced one of the finalists from "America's Got Talent." What we learned from these well-attended happenings is that donors appreciate a first-class event that isn't cost-prohibitive and puts the fun back into raising funds. They also made a significant amount of money for the charity.

We live in an era of reimagining how we do things. Remember the fun you experienced when you went to the circus or a concert? Now imagine that feeling with your fundraisers, and your supporters will enjoy giving to you.

CHAPTER FORTY-FIVE
Crossing the Rubicon

In every industry, there are red lines we don't cross, and the field of development is no exception. Every so often, it is important to review the limiting boundaries and be retold that development professionals must hold themselves to a higher ethical and moral standard because of the august work we do. The public expects no less, and we should do no less.

I liken this philosophy to a story that occurred when my mother, OBM, began to fail mentally. She was a warm and trusting woman who suffered through the Holocaust and was liberated from the concentration camp of Auschwitz. Despite her travails, she managed to keep her sanity and still preserved an innate belief in the goodness of mankind. She felt everyone was decent and trustworthy unless proven otherwise.

In her later years, when her faculties began to decline, her rational reasoning turned irrational. She turned out to be overly trusting to the point where deceiving her was not only possible but also probable. A stranger somehow befriended her and convinced her to bring her bankbooks to the local bank where she held her savings. The two approached a teller in the bank.

The quick-thinking teller recognized my mother and notified the branch manager at once. The miscreant had convinced my mother to withdraw her life savings and hand it over to him. Fortunately, the bank manager intervened just in time, and the wrongdoer fled the bank empty-handed. My mother was flustered, but couldn't understand why all the fuss.

This may be an extreme example, but to me it is a critical point for fundraising professionals to ponder. There are times when donors innocently involve professionals in their personal affairs. This sometimes includes preoccupation with their financial matters. This is different than helping them set up a bequest to the charity. The latter usually is fine. Of concern, however, is when the professional gets inappropriately involved in donor investments and other financial holdings that can lead to unwarranted temptations. There also is a fine line between being named an executor in the donor's estate versus having this handled by a family member or lay leader. There is a timeworn saying that "free cheese is always available in mouse traps." Need I say more?

There are even more egregious matters to avoid when getting too involved with a contributor. Schemes have been set up by unscrupulous scoundrels to launder funds. Simply put, the charity is not a vehicle to make major gifts and then have the bulk of the money returned to the donor because you want to do the donor a favor while also benefiting you or the charity. It's fraud, and it's a crime. Period. Full stop. Actresses Lori Loughlin and Felicity Huffman were caught in money laundering schemes perpetrated by the colleges in which their daughters were to attend. They were convicted and imprisoned.

The three no's you don't discuss with philanthropists—sex, politics and religion—are joined by a fourth—illegal or unethical ways of how to contribute to the nonprofit.

The code of ethical standards issued by the Association of Fundraising Professionals addresses "Public Trust, Transparency & Conflicts of Interest."

Among ethical firewalls, it cites the following: "...not exploit any relationship with a donor prospect, volunteer, client or employee for the benefit of the members or the members' organizations." Don't ask for trouble because, believe me, it will find you and haunt you.

There are other personal matters that are non-financial in nature that development professionals also should avoid becoming involved with for reasons that make them less than proper. One professional I know was asked by a prospect to join him in supplying clean needles in a needle exchange program for drug addicts. Your opinion may be pro or con concerning such programs. But getting involved in such an endeavor may not go over well with others in your community or with leadership of the charity who hear about it. Always think through the consequences.

The title of this chapter is "Crossing the Rubicon." Folks about to make bad decisions are sometimes warned to avoid crossing the Rubicon. What is the meaning behind this phrase? It goes back in history to the time of Julius Caesar who crossed the Rubicon river and precipitated the Roman Civil War that lasted five years and created great turmoil.

It also means that the die is cast and there is no turning back. If history is any prologue to the future, crossing the Rubicon is like the red line you never want to step over.

STRATEGIC
FUNDRAISING
GROUP LLC

CHAPTER FORTY-SIX
Are You the Fly in the Bottle?

A famous Austrian-British philosopher by the name of Ludwig Josef Johann Wittgenstein was regarded by many as the preeminent thinker of the twentieth century. His works primarily delved into matters of logic, mathematics, language and the philosophy of the mind. He lived a life of seclusion in a hut in Norway and was considered a charismatic cult figure.

Wittgenstein famously wrote in his second book titled *Philosophical Investigations* that the aim of his philosophy was "to show the fly the way out of the fly bottle." His observation was a direct attack on the parochial approaches philosophers take and then entangle themselves in their own knotty problems.

The line was inspired by a habit Viennese pub owners had of putting empty beer bottles upside down under the bar. They attracted flies into the bottle who then wouldn't be able to fly back out even after the bottle was put right side up. Instead, they knocked themselves silly as they banged into the bottom of the bottle, or tried to escape by slamming into the glass sides of the bottle until exhausted, and then died. All they had to do was look up and exit the way they flew in.

All of us, and this is true among fundraisers, often have the answer at our fingertips, but we haven't bothered to "look up" to see the solution. We often face complexities or difficulties in life and frequently find that the answer was staring us in the face all along. Yet our myopic attitude sometimes gets in the way, and we keep banging against the bottle and get stuck in a rut, like punctured tires flattened by potholes on a cratered road.

As a nursing home administrator, I once belonged to a trade association of peers and colleagues that regularly faced perplexing issues like mine. It would have been simple enough to throw my hands up in despair on many occasions and give up when challenged by a vexing problem. Instead, I would pick up the phone and call a fellow executive who held the answer to my question. Or I would call professionals that knew me at the trade association who offered promising solutions.

As a senior development executive, I was confronted with simple problems such as finding alternative venues for receptions to dealing with complex political dilemmas such as seating two philanthropists with bad blood between them at the same table at a posh gala. Talking to a colleague or an associate would be my way of looking up and flying out of the bottle. As a member of the Association of Fundraising Professionals (AFP), there are unlimited resources one can turn to get answers.

Early in my career, one of my mentors constantly reminded me that "we are only limited by our creativity." When you think you have seen or done it all, you haven't. You just must look in the right places. Without seeming overly cliché like, there are "many ways to skin a cat" (why anyone would want to skin a cat is beyond me, but that is the saying). Asking lay leadership, committee chairs and committee members is always helpful, and you gain great insights. Conducting your due diligence is another.

Studies purportedly show that when you lose or misplace objects like your keys, most of the time they are within six feet of where you last saw the items. All you must do is look in the right place, and you will find them. Sometimes it is just a matter of looking up (or around), because even if they're not in the exact same location, it may jog your memory to their whereabouts.

Albert Einstein was said to have coined the saying, "The definition of insanity is doing the same thing over and over again expecting different results." How often do we find ourselves doing just that? We repeat the same mistakes, but expect different results, just like the fly in the bottle. Sometimes, it's just a question of putting on our inventor's hat and going about solving a problem in a different way to get to the answer.

There is a relevant story told in Exodus 17; 8-16. It is the skirmish in the desert between Joshua and the Amalekites. The Amalekites were the sworn enemy of the Israelites and never fought fair. It is said that Moses was on the hilltop overlooking the battle below. When he raised his hands to Heaven, Joshua and his troops triumphed. But when Moses became weary and his hands lowered, the Amalekites prevailed. What brought victory to Joshua was when Aaron and Hur had Moses sit on a stone and hold up Moses' hands.

In his book *Lessons in Leadership* the late Rabbi Lord Jonathan Sacks offered this noteworthy interpretation of that story. He suggested what brought on the victory was Joshua and his fighters looking up to Heaven and seeing Moses keep his hands raised. Looking up inspired the Israelites to win the fight. While raising Moses' hands was critical to the battle, so too were the combatants looking up to overcome their enemies with the spiritual armaments they needed.

So, when you are confounded by a problem, don't become twisted in knots. Remember, the bottle is open; your way out just may be to look up.

STRATEGIC FUNDRAISING GROUP LLC

CHAPTER FORTY-SEVEN
Creating a Meaningful Legacy

Alfred Nobel was the inventor of dynamite. One day he was reading the newspaper, and his jaw dropped when, unexpectedly, he read his own obituary. In the startling obit, he was named the "Dynamite King," a title he didn't want to be remembered by. He later learned that the notice of his demise was meant for his brother who had recently went on to meet his Maker. A journalist had erred and written about the wrong Nobel. Nevertheless, it bothered him that he might be remembered for something so violent.

He resolved that day to change the path his life had taken and, instead, to dedicate himself and his massive fortune to creating five yearly prizes that are known worldwide as the Nobel Prize in the fields of peace, physics, chemistry, medicine and literature. Nobel is remembered not for creating weapons of destruction, but instead for exalting impactful contributions to human knowledge. That became his meaningful legacy.

The broad definition of a legacy is something that gets passed down from one generation to the next, which often involves assets of some kind such as property or even just money, an inheritance. But it also can involve passing down an individual's or institution's reputation. Over the centuries, Jewish sages were preoccupied with preserving one's reputation. *Ethics of our Fathers* (4:13) has a beautiful adage that applies so well in this instance: "Rabbi Shimon asserts: 'There are three crowns—the crown of Torah, the crown of priesthood and the crown of monarchy—but the crown of a good name outweighs them all.'"

One can be an extraordinary scholar or even descend from an impeccable lineage. But the rabbis suggested that having a sterling ranking surpasses even the finest scholarly background or high-brow ancestry. Both *Proverbs* (22:1) and *Ecclesiastes* (7:1) each allude to the fact that a good name is more precious than fine oil or costly perfume. So, creating and sustaining an untarnished legacy is a fundamental imperative in life.

The story of Alfred Nobel is germane because the anecdote applies to both nonprofits and development professionals alike. The most noble (no pun intended) aspiration of any not-for-profit organization and its professional leadership is to pursue a legacy of excellence based on integrity, accomplishment and quality service. How you are remembered is a function of what you achieved during a lifespan of honesty, transparency and quality services.

A person's legacy is often appraised as a work in progress and not just what is left at the end of a lifetime. How nonprofits and their leaders treat their supporters and those they serve is factored into their legacy in progress as well as what they tangibly leave to the next generation. Today, a cottage industry has sprung up to clear up blemished reputations or those sullied by poor reviews on the Internet or, worse, by scandal. However, no form of historical expurgation can shore up the legacy of nonprofits or their leadership if they don't uphold honest reputations.

The business world is littered with a preponderance of companies whose reputations were ruined like trampled cigarette butts on sidewalks in front of college dormitories before finals. The difference is that for-profit companies can typically salvage their reputations; nonprofits find it more challenging. Here are some examples of proprietary companies that mounted huge comebacks despite overwhelming odds against their recoveries:

1) In 1982, seven Chicago residents died when someone laced their Extra-Strength Tylenol with cyanide. Nowadays, it is estimated that Johnson & Johnson is a $44 billion company with strong projected growth.

2) In 1993, a syringe found in a can of Pepsi sent PepsiCo careening into a near-death roll. These days, it's a more-than-$70-billion company expecting continued growth.

3) In 2010, an underwater oil spill made BP the most hated company in America. At the moment, it is nearly a $280 billion company positioned for major growth in a cyclical industry.

Charity scandals that have rocked the nonprofit world include charities such as the Wounded Warrior Project (money allegedly spent on parties and hobbies), the Moore Charitable Foundation ($25 million invested in fraudulent investment schemes) and even the Leonardo DiCaprio Foundation (part of a major embezzlement scandal), and the list grows. Tarnishing one's reputation clouds over all the good these and other charities achieve and hurts innocent charities in the process.

Warren Buffet once said, "It takes 20 years to build a reputation and five minutes to ruin it. If you think about that, you'll do things differently." And this is why burnishing your good name with creditworthy achievements is the means to your ultimate legacy.

STRATEGIC
FUNDRAISING
GROUP LLC

CHAPTER FORTY-EIGHT
Fundraising in the Year 2075

I am not a crystal ball gazer, but, sometimes, it is fun to prognosticate. It has been a hobby of mine to predict future trends that could change the field of development. My accuracy, however, is wholly contingent on how influencing factors come together. But let's have some fun with some of my predictions.

Basic Building Blocks

During the next fifty years, the basic fundraising building blocks such as major gifts, special events, direct mail, web campaigns, annual and capital giving, grassroots altruism, planned gifts such as bequests and endowment fund giving should remain intact. What will probably change is how funds are allocated into their respective buckets.

The Donor Experience

A paradigm shift is already taking place and will continue over the next half century. The Baby Boom generation will fade away, and aging Millennials will change the current thinking about how and why to give to charities. Most Baby Boomers once were happy with just writing a check, getting a plaque or special premium in return and giving the charity carte blanche on how to use its funds. That will change dramatically as donors assert a brawnier role in how their money is spent.

Technology

As the cost of new and innovative technologies decrease, their use will increase concomitantly.

The International Space Station will see tourists visiting on a regular basis. According to CNBC, as of 2020, NASA was charging a mere $52 to $55 million for a stayover. Even as this book was being written, hundreds and hundreds of adventurers were signing up for a measly pittance, about $250,000, for joyrides into outer space with Sir Richard Branson, Elon Musk or Jeff Bezos type of spaceships. So, the notion of space tourism for charity is not far-fetched, nor out of reach for the wealthy explorer. *To boldly go where no one has gone before.*

During the writing of this book, Virgin Galactic founded by Sir Richard Branson announced a sweepstakes that would give the prizewinner two seats aboard one of the first commercial flights to outer space. Anyone was eligible to enter for free, but the sponsor sought donations to Space for Humanity, a charity making spaceflight more reachable for the consumer. *May the force be with you!*

As these trips become more cost-efficient, expect that enterprising charities will arrange for philanthropists or their designates to stay there in exchange for making substantial contributions to their nonprofit. In time, ion rocket engines using light or warp speed will quickly reach the Moon, Mars and other planets, and similar arrangements will be made for the itinerant voyager. Someday, expect trendy receptions in these exotic locations. *Hello, Hal.*

Holograms will play a more prominent role in the future. Holograms surround us now, but most people don't even know it. Among items with holograms on them today include driver's licenses, identification cards, credit cards, DVD and Blu-ray players, software packaging and much more. However, expect that, in the future, 3D hologram images of leadership and a motley of philanthropic projects will be transmitted virtually to innumerable locations where, for example, even in the comfort of one's own home, donors will learn about important initiatives directly in front of them. They will then interact with the lay leader's and/or professional's tangible image. *Beam me up, Scotty.*

The Bill and Melinda Gates Foundation issued a report on using artificial intelligence (AI) for fundraising and philanthropy. We learned that there are already many AI uses taking place. We also know that you, I and most donors want to communicate directly with a human and not an automated voice. However, there is not always a human being on hand at a moment's notice to talk to a supporter. The closest, therefore, will be something akin to Amazon's Alexa or Apple's Siri. Prescient virtual chatbots and human-like androids will be increasingly available to serve as conversational interfaces between persons and the organization. *"I, Robot," move over.*

My grandson Sammy introduced me to Oculus Quest 2, an amazing immersive virtual reality technology. After donning a pair of goggles that look more like a deep-sea diver's mask, you become immersed in a totally different world. You are encouraged to be very careful as you enter different environments because you can, literally, lose your balance if not careful. This technology covers a wide array of environments of your own creation or that are made for you. My point—future fundraising will take this technology to a new level, when wearing the unconventional-looking spectacles will give nonprofits unlimited possibilities of bringing directly to donors environments they can touch and feel. This will make the giving experience more tangible and realistic, especially for those unable to personally visit a facility or program. As Mr. Spock might say, "Fascinating."

Donor Recognition via Evolving Technologies

Special opportunities for donors to express their esteem for a loved one or to commemorate a celebration or milestone occasion will evolve to a new level. The novel technology will allow donors to give family and friends *anywhere* in the world, even on another planet, a way to see the dedication.

Many not-for-profit organizations do not have the physical facilities to mount a donor wall, or do not have the ability to offer dedications or commemorations to their donors. Other organizations may have such options, but cannot add to them or are looking for a method to allow donors living anywhere in the world, or on another planet, a way to view the commemoration. Enter the virtual donor recognition system (VDRS).

The VDRS will consist of an Internet-based donor recognition system that will offer not-for-profit organizations a way to tangibly recognize donations by contributors. Donors will commemorate occasions, or dedicate a virtual plaque in honor of a loved one, friend or anyone, or memorialize a loved one, friend or anyone on an exclusively designed virtual donor wall (e.g., Tree of Life, Wall of Remembrance or Garden of Memories). Commemorations will be possible with basic inscriptions, or enhanced with still images and/or video clips. These also will be projected as tangible holographic images anywhere.

The VDRS will be accessible on a new type of upgraded Internet (yet to be invented) in a manner that will distinguish it from the conventional dedication wall. Families and friends of donors will be able to access the dedication worldwide, or even on another planet, giving this form of dedication an advantage over other more conventional formats. Thus, families and all donors will be able to access a view of the commemoration without having to be present where the physical wall may be situated, if there is a wall at all. The holographic image will have a touchable, physical texture to it, a technology that does not yet exist today. *Thank you, 3-CPO.*

Caveat, Emptor; Charities, Beware!

A word of caution about my speculations. The state of the economy commonly affects philanthropic contributions. If the economy falters, as it did during the COVID-19 pandemic, all bets are off. My outlook for the US economy is a pessimistic one for a major reason. Our politicians in Washington have placed the burden of unbearable debt upon the shoulders of this nation—annual deficits are in the trillions, and we are drowning in debt—and it may lead to a crushing financial crash heretofore unseen. And we may not have to wait fifty years to experience this financial calamity.

Our national debt is climbing faster than a SpaceX rocket heading into orbit. In my view, a "pox on both houses," because both major political parties have buried this nation in a quagmire of unlimited borrowing and ceaseless spending, but tax revenues and other forms of income are not matching the outgo. Politicians are printing paper from the US Mint like it was Monopoly money. And because they have created a pathology of welfare dependency in the country, the future is ominous. It's not a question of whether but when the tipping point will be reached, and our feckless politicians will throw the country off a fiscal cliff. Charitable institutions be forewarned. Sorry for the gloomy outlook, but eventually the piper will come calling. How's that Venezuelan toilet paper working out?

Change in our Way of Thinking

People are generally complacent about change, or don't like it. Like us, institutions are creatures of habit and are used to carrying out fund-raising activities a certain way—just like the famous song in *Fiddler on the Roof*, "Tradition." The resourceful nonprofit, however, will shake the 8-ball for answers and, like a chameleon changing colors, alter the way it does business.

And let's not forget what a famous football coach used to proclaim: "The future is now." Can the Holodeck from *Star Trek* be far behind? *Greetings, Data.*

CHAPTER FORTY-NINE
Raising Money from the Dead

Raising money from the dead . . . well, it's like raising money from the dead. Certainly, a challenge, but not an insurmountable one. And, no, we refer not to the days of Mashiach (Hebrew for "the Messiah"). We are talking about here and now. Truthfully, though, we raise money *for* the dead and not *from* them.

An article in *The Jewish Link of New Jersey* not long ago headlined "Jewish Cemeteries Rescue Group Plans Inaugural Gala" pointed to the sad fact that "there are dozens of Jewish cemeteries in the tri-state area that have significantly deteriorated, many in need of dire restoration." Being that burial grounds are considered consecrated sites in Judaism, and they are the eternal resting places of family, friends and our brethren, the neglect of these graveyards should be both disturbing and heartbreaking to all of us.

My wife and I visited cemeteries in Poland and Hungary where many in her ancestry are buried, especially family that lived in Eastern Europe before and during WWII. It was a matter of infinite dismay to see the decaying conditions of many cemeteries in Europe. In the Warsaw Cemetery, for example, some four hundred and fifty thousand people are buried, but the cemetery is in dreary shape. Unfortunately, cemeteries around the world in places as far-flung as Prague, the Czech Republic, Ukraine, Russia, Bukovina, Galicia, Czernowitz and even in the near and far East also are in deplorable condition.

Countless cemeteries represent a vanished world, yet a vibrant and colorful one that once existed and now is mostly forgotten. The Jewish communities that once thrived in shtetls (Yiddish for "villages") where the cemeteries are found were either killed, died out or moved away. Now, only an occasional caretaker, if any, is around to watch over crumbling gravestones. Fortunately, there seems to be a renewed effort by various volunteer groups to visit and clean up unkempt and decrepit sites. But the need cries out for more help and support.

An organization once hired me to provide consulting advice and counsel on raising funds for the maintenance and increased security needs of the Mount of Olives (Har Hazeitim) in Israel, the oldest surviving Jewish cemetery in the world. Jews have been buried there since biblical times and, among others, it houses the tombs and final resting spots for some of the most prominent Jewish personages of antiquity through the modern era. Located in the Holy Land, it is far removed from Jews around the world and, therefore, it's challenging to raise money for its diverse needs.

Muddying matters are the political hurdles to overcome. The environment in which the Mount of Olives finds itself includes a powerful Sacred (Burial) Society (Chevra Kadisha) and splinter burial societies that lay claim to the operations of the mountain, a hostile Arab and Mosque presence that cause regular disruptions including the stoning of visitors as well as the erratic partisan involvement of Knesset ministers whose competing political needs can affect vital funding support. All these influences complicate the fundraising for this famous mountain. But fundraising tools were created and recommended, including unique commemorative opportunities, various sponsorships, special events and individual and corporate membership programs. It can be done there and elsewhere.

In South Florida, Rabbi Jay Lyons, Director, took on the task of setting up the South Florida Jewish Cemetery, a nonprofit endeavor, to encourage traditional Jewish burials for any Jew of any background. Under the aegis of NASCK (National Association of Chevra Kadisha), not only did it acquire the land, but on an ongoing basis seeks funding through web solicitations and other appeals. It also provides a proper funeral and monument for any indigent Jew who needs one. The idea is to support an authentic and affordable green Jewish burial and not cremation, considered an anathema to traditional orthodox Jewish practice.

The nonprofit Community Alliance for Jewish-affiliated Cemeteries (CAJAC) also was mentioned in the above cited *Jewish Link* story and is committed to restoring cemeteries in disrepair located in New Jersey and New York. It too has an executive director and a board of directors overseeing its sacred work. CAJAC handled the restoration of the Bayside Cemetery in Ozone Park, Queens, which was founded in 1865. Its inaugural gala was just one way to fund its essential services.

Volunteer groups or individuals throughout the world are taking on the holy mission of restoring innumerable cemeteries in desperate need of rescue or remediation. Avigdor Sharon, an Israeli citizen, took on the duty of restoring the local Jewish cemetery in Beled, Hungary, a small town inhabited by many Jews before WWII, but where none or few are left today. One of his primary motivators was that many family members are buried there. He was a one-man marching band who got the job done by personally soliciting major philanthropists in America, Canada, England, Israel and elsewhere to raise the required funds.

So, can funding be raised for even desolate cemeteries here and around the world? Absolutely. It's definitely not a dead issue.

CHAPTER FIFTY
Learning from the Best

Wikipedia defines a best practice as "a method or technique that has been generally accepted as superior to any alternatives because it produces results that are superior to those achieved by other means or because it has become a standard way of doing things." That is the working proposition for this chapter and, in my estimation, a practical way of putting it.

Many of us are taught early in life and later at work to learn from the best. Learn from the role models, "they" say. Not sure who "they" are, but "they" must know. We always are encouraged to choose the best practices to follow in virtually any industry or line of work. This holds true for industries as far ranging as human resource management to the sciences and medicine to social media to public policy to fundraising and so forth. For many, this approach is just plain common sense. We are, thusly, urged to follow the best practices of successful leaders or organizations and be like them.

In the field of fundraising, we often look to larger successful organizations and try to learn from their best practices, and then apply what we learned to moderately sized and smaller institutions. However, there are times when pure luck strikes, and while efforts are made to duplicate unique results, at best, we can only emulate what others have done more effectively. A good example is the ALS Ice Bucket Challenge that came about in 2014 (see the chapter called "Successful Fundraisers: Just Luck or Something More?").

Initially, the aim of the ALS Ice Bucket Challenge was just to promote awareness of the disease amyotrophic lateral sclerosis (ALS), but it became an instant viral hit and raised upwards of $220 million worldwide. Yet, it met with mixed results by others, large and small, who imitated the challenge. Some fared well; some didn't. The following year, the ALS organization itself tried to establish the challenge as an annual event, but it no longer held the same novelty as the year before and, eventually, tailed off.

So, who are the nonprofit fundraising giants from whom to learn best practices as we model our development activities after them? It is helpful to separate these into the following general categories:

1) Religious
2) Health care
3) Academic/Education
4) Social services

Depending on where your organization falls may generally determine what best practices you wish to take away. It's not an exact science, but like a compass in a large forest of trees, looking at what role models do gives you a sense of direction and where you should be headed.

A myriad of organizations generally fall under each of these categories. Let's exclude those in the proprietary sector such as investment fundraising or the political arena where politicians thrive on a different fundraising dynamic. Accordingly, this is the most important sentence in this chapter: *The first place to start and find out what works for them is by visiting their websites that will give you a sense immediately of how they raise money.* Look for their annual reports and giving literature, and you will learn even more.

Space limits our ability to present an exhaustive analysis of institutions in each category, but it behooves us to name some in each category that we believe offer imaginative ideas anyone can use. This is purely subjective, and anyone can develop their own list. The idea, however, is to shine the light on a few productive organizations from whom we can learn a thing or two. This chapter is not intended to discuss their flagship activities, just identify several organizations whom you can research. The next steps are up to you.

Under the Religious category, I would recommend researching Catholic Charities USA, Lutheran Services in America, the UJA, Jewish Federations, Chabad-Lubavitch and similar entities.

Under Health care, examine agencies under the large medical systems such as Mount Sinai Health Systems, St. Jude Children's Research Hospital, Task Force for Global Health and major disease organizations such as the American Cancer Society, American Heart Association and the like.

Under Academic/Education, check on Step Up for Students and look at the major universities of higher learning such as Harvard, Yale or Princeton, especially under their alumni and endowment fund activities.

Under Social services, consider researching organizations such as Habitat for Humanity, Boys & Girls Clubs of America, Goodwill Industries, Red Cross and many more.

Are there outliers who don't neatly fit under these categories? Of course, there are, and these include United Way Worldwide, Feeding America, YMCA of the USA and others like them. Remember, I said this wasn't an exhaustive list.

A word about originality—every organization should foster pioneering thinking and nurture or incubate novel fundraising projects that harbor great potential for excellent results. If we don't do so, then we won't achieve cutting-edge innovations that drive our nonprofits to financial success.

CHAPTER FIFTY-ONE
What About Planned Giving?

This is the story about the one that almost got away, but didn't.

No, this isn't a story about a fishing adventure, albeit the analogy is a good one. It's an account of why treating your donors with respect and dignity is a fundamental rule and, if sincere, can pay off handsomely.

When I became director of development at a nonprofit in Brooklyn, New York, I made it a top priority to be introduced to each member of the board of directors. While board members wanted to know who I was and what my expectations were, I wanted to discern what was on their minds. It was an opportunity to survey the board concerning their feelings about the organization. It was an invaluable experience. It was like doing a mini-feasibility survey.

During my visits with each board member, we discussed not only their state of mind about the organization, but also their confidence in, or lack thereof, of our planned $16 million capital campaign. As you would expect, their opinions ranged from an overconfident to a pessimistic view of the campaign. Clearly, a lot of groundwork had to be laid patiently to create an atmosphere of confidence, but not by way of extremes.

This story is about a director, a lay leader, who had been associated with the institution for at least forty years. She was a reserved, although not timid, individual who had been generous, but not overly generous, and certainly reached nowhere close to her philanthropic potential. Our meeting turned out to be fortuitous because she was ready to quit the board. As we got to know each other, she developed trust in me, especially since she knew that I was authentic in my intentions, had the right abilities and was genuinely concerned about the best interests of the infirmed residents whom she loved.

There are two critical obstacles every fundraiser must overcome when developing a relationship with a donor. The first is *trust*. To connect with the prospective contributor, the fundraiser must first establish a sense of utter trustworthiness. Unless the donor has absolute confidence in the fundraiser, the relationship goes nowhere.

The second obstacle to overcome is connecting the donor with the *mission* of the organization. Otherwise, you may have a nice trusting relationship, but if the donor can't relate to the nonprofit's calling, then the spark of interest won't ignite when you need to kindle the flame.

Back to the director—she was already connected to the institution's mission as shown by her forty-year commitment. What lacked for the moment was her trust in me. It is a lengthy matter to describe how I earned her trust and confidence. What is important is that a lot of hand holding was necessary to move her from a *bad place* to a *good place*. It didn't happen overnight, and it was a steady and drawn-out process. It frequently is.

Her most importunate disenchantment was attributable to the lack of respect and dignity the board accorded her, especially considering her long-time involvement and open-ended charitable inclinations. Sadly, she suppressed a strong resentment and bitterness towards the board leadership and, more alarmingly, to the very institution she was prepared to abandon because of her disillusionment. Her input wasn't valued at board meetings, and there were many instances when she wasn't even invited. Her departure would have triggered an immense financial loss for the organization unless we turned things around.

It became my role to act as intermediary with the CEO, president and board to assuage her hurt feelings and reconcile her with some of the board members who didn't show her the respect she was due. So, we made sure to promote her favorite resident activities such as distributing ice cream on Mother's Day to all the ladies on every nursing unit. We involved her in the planning of the annual gala, which she looked forward to and enjoyed. She was instrumental in founding an art gallery on one of the wings in the facility. Before long, she once again became a strong spokesperson for the institution to her many affluent friends. That by itself resulted in a small windfall.

Her renewed enthusiasm resulted in a $250,000 gift to establish a cultural center in the facility and a much larger naming gift for our showcase Solarium. Other contributions flowed in, too, from her and her many friends. Joy was soon restored in Mudville!

By now you must be asking, "What does this have to do with planned giving?" Good question, and the answer is as follows. Once things were patched up, I spent considerable time discussing with her the benefit of leaving a bequest to the organization. It was after her passing that we learned she bequeathed $5 million to the institution!

CHAPTER FIFTY-TWO
The Value of a
Good Commemoration

The word on the street is that commemorations in the form of plaques (physical and digital), monuments of different shapes and sizes or the naming of buildings or programs are passe. Newer contributors, such as the Millennial generation, are said to frown on these methods of donor recognition. My empirical observations lead me to believe otherwise. Commemorations are here to stay, but over time their prominence may diminish. Kid yourself not, however, because there are donors who value good commemorations for very personal reasons, especially on buildings.

One top professional I know came up with what some might consider a brilliant commemoration; others may be repelled by the idea. Let's call our top fundraiser, David, and we'll call the philanthropist, Jack. As the beneficiary of this commemoration, it meant the world to the philanthropist. But, first, this story requires a prefacing explanation.

Jack and his wife, Doris, were an affluent couple who lived in Manhattan, New York, and later moved to South Florida. Both became involved with an Israeli-based organization through a series of circumstances not significant to this story. What is pertinent is that they were firmly engaged by David, and they became enamored with him and his organization.

Stewardship is an important part of the cycle of keeping consistent contact with donors, retaining them and keeping them engaged with the nonprofit. It has been my experience that unengaged donors become disengaged donors. And then they go elsewhere. That's why a meaningful stewardship program usually results in further gifts to the organization.

Back to the story—Doris became seriously ill. David pulled out all the stops and, literally, camped out in their home. David gave new meaning to the term "stewardship."

David brought the couple food, he ran errands for them and, when he couldn't be there, he sent an emissary to stand in for him and continue to take care of all their personal needs. When Doris passed, he made all the arrangements for the funeral, even officiated at the burial, and took care of post-funeral activities such as Shiva and ordering the monument for Doris with an original inscription he composed. Jack was most grateful.

For years following her death, David stayed in regular touch with Jack. At the time, I worked for another nonprofit and, ironically, when David or his emissary left Jack's company, I usually was Jack's next visitor. I stayed in regular touch with Jack and preserved a close connection with him to sustain the long-term relationship my organization also had with him. There were times when I left Jack, and lo and behold, David or his emissary arrived for another visit. Our calendars were practically synchronized for these visits. It became a running joke.

Jack was getting older and frailer. David dreamt up an idea that, in my view, was truly inspired, although I know some will disagree. He regularly had invited Jack to Israel, but Jack hesitated because he was concerned about the lengthy trips back and forth. So, David produced this brainstorm. He planted a monument on the grounds of the orga-nization identical to Doris's gravestone, inscription and all. When

Jack arrived in Israel, David shepherded him everywhere, took care of his lodging and food and eventually took him to visit his nonprofit.

When Jack arrived and saw the monument, he filled with emotion and his eyes welled up with tears. What greeted him next was an uplifting ceremony held at the site of his wife's replica gravestone. Psalms were recited, David eulogized Doris, a children's choir sang and a special plaque presentation was made to Jack that just "blew him away." Jack was extremely grateful to David for this unique observance on Doris' yahrzeit (Yiddish for "the anniversary date of death"). Ultimately, this program with all its trappings resulted in another seven-figure gift to the institution. It also occasioned a major bequest after Jack passed. Mission complete!

David's idea of creating a duplicate gravestone in Israel for Doris that was dedicated on her yahrzeit was a stroke of genius. It also was how David enticed Jack to take the lengthy and wearisome trip to Israel. But Jack was glad he went, and when he returned home, I, and all of Jack's friends, got to see the ceremony that was filmed and presented to Jack on a DVD during David's next trip to the United States. It now exists in the archives of fundraising history.

As professionals, we often grapple with deciding what borders on good taste versus bad taste. This applies to a commemoration that might be looked at as excessive, but in the eyes of the donor might be considered fitting.

So, was David's idea too outlandish or inappropriate? In my judgment, the results speak for themselves.

CHAPTER FIFTY-THREE
The Lynchpin

The lynchpin in a nonprofit plays an incredibly pivotal role in the growth and development of the organization. He or she is, or should be, a professional well versed in the inner workings of the nonprofit. The lynchpin also cements relationships with the public and philanthropic associations, as well as the nonprofit community. The professional fundraiser often plays the role of the lynchpin, as do other key faces representing the organization.

Early in my nursing home administrator's career, I held membership in a trade association called the National Association of Jewish Homes and Housing for the Aging (NAJHHA) and was privileged to receive its first Dr. Herbert Shore Young Administrator of the Year award. The recognition reflected my service in nursing home administration and my assignment as the editor of the NAJHHA national newsletter and magazine. It put me in the forefront of the public eye on many fronts. In essence, I had the ability to represent my trade and become a lynchpin to various publics such as folks in national communities seeking information about long-term care facilities for their loved ones, vendors who sought economic connections and philanthropists with issues that needed personal attention.

As my career evolved into my becoming a senior development executive, I acted in a similar capacity when representing my employers. Serving as a liaison doesn't mean that the development professional always has his or her mind on raising funds. On the contrary, just conserving convivial relationships with donors as part of the cultivation process is equally important. Keeping a reservoir of relatable stories to share with contributors is crucial to relationship building. Here is an example that led to some nice charitable gifts.

As a NAJHHA member, I often attended national conferences either to learn about recent innovations in the field and/or enhance my general knowledge. There also were seminars in which I was the facilitator or instructor. This story revolves around a program one year in New Orleans at which I presented. It's a true anecdote that was helpful to me later when I became a senior development executive.

There is an adage that the way to a man's heart is through his stomach. But perhaps, it's also the way to a generous philanthropist through a good story. The NAJHHA conference I attended took place at the Sheraton Metairie in Louisiana. The association brought in a mashgiach (Hebrew for "kosher supervisor") for all the meal functions. I had known the mashgiach for many years as he was a close family friend from Connecticut. One of the banquet meals highlighted a Cajun-style roast beef dinner that was beyond delicious. It was amazingly delectable.

I asked the mashgiach whether he knew the recipe for this gourmet dinner. It turned out he was a close friend of the executive chef. A few minutes later, he took me into the main kitchen and introduced me to Chef Rousseau who, sporting a black handlebar mustache and a thick French accent, whisked me around on a royal tour of the kitchen. The next part of the visit was discovering the exquisite recipe for the Cajun-style roast beef. His secret was in marinating the meat in a cooler for twenty-four hours using special seasoning and an original sauce that the chef conjured up. I tucked that recipe away for future reference.

After the tour by Chef Rousseau, the mashgiach took my wife and me to a Melba Toast factory, which in itself was fascinating because we saw multi-level assembly lines and conveyor belts bearing Melba Toast type products being packaged by a half dozen different companies. What interested me was that only some of the products with identical ingredients, but different brand names, enjoyed kosher supervision. The origination process was the same, but the mashgiach only provided approval to a select few companies whose product was labeled with the kosher symbol.

So, now that you followed my journey to New Orleans, you must be asking yourself, *What does this have to do with fundraising?* Good question, and here is the answer. These food-related episodes fared me well later in my development career when I bonded with a philanthropist in the food business. He was absolutely enthralled with the story of Chef Rousseau and wanted to know all the intimate details about the Sheraton Metairie's kitchen, including the equipment used by the gourmet chef and his private Cajun-style recipe. He also was captivated by my visit to the Melba Toast factory and fascinated by its kosher supervision policy. It established my long-term relationship with the donor and solidified my becoming his lynchpin to the organization.

Being the lynchpin of your nonprofit carries noteworthy responsibility. Keep this in mind as food for thought.

CHAPTER FIFTY-FOUR
How Appealing Are You?

It was an innocent phone call and it went something like this:

Me: "Hi, Joe. Glad I was able to reach you. Thanks for taking my call. It's that time of the year again when we schedule an appeal for my organization at (the name of synagogue). Can you schedule us in your calendar?"

Joe: "Sure. No problem. Give me a minute while I pull out my calendar."

(I waited for a few minutes, with sounds of car horns and the sound of several voices in the background).

Joe: "Thanks for waiting. It's marked on the calendar. Don't worry."

Me: "Thank you so much, Joe. When shall I contact you to discuss what materials to bring with me to the appeal?"

Joe: "Call me in a week. I can't really talk now. I am on my way to my wife's funeral."

True story.

While this really happened, it isn't always so easy to arrange synagogue appeals. But it can be done, and nonprofits often overlook this not-so-insignificant way to raise indispensable funds as part of an overall fundraising program. I was privileged to raise major funds for one organization each year at various synagogues in the New York metropolitan area, in Florida and in California at scheduled times during Sabbath or Holiday services. I ran eight to ten minute appeals.

It is written in the Torah that as the Jews wandered in the desert, Moses solicited the children of Israel towards the construction of the portable Tabernacle called the Mishkan. Eventually, he stopped them from giving half shekels because he raised more than enough funding to complete the task. I don't know of any nonprofits who exclaim, "Stop, stop! We have enough money. No more!" Nevertheless, Moses' method of appeal works.

Fundraising appeals are certainly not limited to any specific religion. Every day in synagogues and churches everywhere, someone passes around a charity plate or walks around with a charity box asking congregants to pitch in and help with the financial needs of the institution. Holiday appeals for different religions often supplement other essential campaigns during the year.

Televangelist John C. Hagee, the founder and senior pastor of Cornerstone Church in San Antonio, Texas, has run innumerable appeals and raised millions of dollars over the years not only for his church but also for Jewish charities. Other evangelists such as the late Billy Graham, his son Franklin, Pat Robertson and Joel Osteen, among many others, run enormously successful appeals on TV, as well as in their respective ministries.

Hospitals, universities, national politicians and large fundraising behemoths have amassed massive fund-laden coffers for their annual campaigns, all due to personal appeals to alumni, patient families, partisan political action committees and the like. These appeals extend from one-on-one approaches to secure major gifts, all the way to mammoth fund drives and major state-by-state crusades held in gigantic stadia.

The annual Chabad Telethon appeals have raised tens of millions of dollars for the important work of Lubavitch. In addition, the UJA and Jewish federations across north America host different forms of appeals (the word appeal is actually embodied in the name UJA, as in United Jewish *Appeal*) that also raise multi-millions for Israel and domestic causes.

So, how does this information help the moderately sized to small nonprofit?

It is worth the effort to explore securing Shabbat and Jewish holiday appeals in synagogues. These are, of course, a challenge to attain, but the effort should be made because they deliver a potentially high rate of return for minimal cost. They are one of the most cost-effective ways of raising funds.

There are different types of synagogue appeals, and these include, but are not limited to, the following that are the most popular:

1) Open appeal
2) Closed appeal
3) Direct mail appeal utilizing the synagogue membership list
4) E-blast appeal to the synagogue membership e-list
5) Modified appeal (pledge cards handed out and collected, but not announced)
6) Rabbinical appeal from the pulpit
7) Newsletter appeal with a page dedicated to the nonprofit

There are different approaches to securing an appeal, and these vary from synagogue to synagogue and program to program. These include, but are not limited to, contacting the key decision makers:

1) Appeals committee
2) Chairman of the appeals committee

3) Owner of the Jewish holiday program
4) President of the synagogue
5) Rabbi of the synagogue
6) Executive committee
7) Board of directors
8) Some combination of the above

What is usually the determining factor in setting up a synagogue appeal? It is addressing this issue: can you show how the nonprofit benefits the congregants or the local community? If you cannot create that connection, then it becomes a bigger challenge to run a successful appeal. Naming a specific Shabbat or Jewish holiday each year that ties into your mission can also help.

This concept is easily transferable to nonprofit churches and mosques everywhere. Obviously, there are inherent differences in how these may be held. That's what the professional is there for. It's doable.

But my question still stands: how appealing are you?

STRATEGIC
FUNDRAISING
GROUP LLC

CHAPTER FIFTY-FIVE
Jabberwocky

Lewis Carroll, whose pseudonym was Charles Ludwidge Dodgson, was a nineteenth-century English children's fiction writer probably best known for his great works *Alice's Adventures in Wonderland* and *Through the Looking-Glass*. However, I remember him best for another one of his fantasy works – the most famous literary nonsense poem of all time called "Jabberwocky."

The first verse always stuck with me, and it goes like this:

'Twas brillig, and the slithy toves
Did gyre and gimble in the wabe:
All mimsy were the borogoves,
And the mome raths outgrabe.

Makes no sense, right? The rest of this epic poem isn't much different. While the linguistic inventiveness was thoroughly analyzed, it remains today as a dish of delightful gobbledygook.

So, what does this have to do with fundraising? Good question. It links well to planned giving, a major building block of fundraising. Let me explain.

Anyone who has dabbled in planned giving programs understands that these do not generally produce immediate results. When meeting with planned giving prospects, the idea is to introduce them to a unique type of charitable gift that benefits them during their lifetime or after. These concepts take time to explain, develop and nurture.

Planned gifts take many forms such as legacies and bequests, charitable gift annuities, charitable trusts of different kinds including lead, annuity and unitrusts, gifts of life insurance, 401(k) and 403(b) retirement plans, IRAs, brokerage accounts and the list goes on.

According to data by the National Philanthropic Trust, giving through bequests alone in 2019 "equaled about 9% of all charitable donations or $43.2 billion" in the United States. This is not inconsequential loose change and represents only legacy gifts, a component of planned giving.

For donors to consider planned gifts, concepts must be marketed to them in ways that are understandable and reveal favorable tax advantages, as well as how assets are preserved for the next generation and even generations thereafter. We all know an uncle by the name of Sam who loves to dip into our wealth estate and take big chunks from it. We don't want that, do we?

You will drool over attractive rates older folks are eligible to receive with, for example, charitable gift annuities. You need only look at some interest rate tables promoted by many nonprofits. The principal inures to the charity following death, but generates income at high interest levels while donors are alive. The rates make you salivate because their rate of return is guaranteed. Unlike stocks and dividends, which can be risky, these rates are safeguarded by the charity. This makes them lucrative to older folks because they are age-based—the older the donor is at the time of purchase, the higher is the rate.

One method I used to market planned giving was to host seminars featuring speakers whose expertise revolved around such financial instruments. The seminars came with the requisite bagels and cream cheese refreshments, as well as free premiums for the senior citizen attendants. We gave away a lot of tote bags with all kinds of goodies inside. Our programs were educational, and also satisfied hunger pangs.

One day, a small group neatly packed up their bagels and pastries into their tote bags and got up to leave the session early. I went over to them and asked why they were leaving. They told me, "There's a UJA federation seminar down the street. We can't be late." Well, that wasn't comforting. Needless to say, we didn't fare well that day.

However, at one program, we sold several sizable charitable gift annuities and realized a $1.3 million unitrust. A unitrust, also known as a charitable remainder trust, is a legal device defined by federal tax law from which the beneficiary annually receives a fixed percentage of the fair market value of its assets. Needless to say, that was a great day for us.

But what does this have to do with Lewis Carroll?

Well, the speaker that day went into a convoluted description of how a unitrust works. He was long-winded, quite elaborate, giving an unusually complex explanation of every possible intricate detail about unitrusts. He lost me and most of our audience. I could see most eyes were glazed over, and I thought to myself, *What a wasted opportunity!*

And then it happened.

An older gentleman wearing a tweed hat, a torn and stained shirt, unlaced tennis shoes and an overcoat reminiscent of Detective Columbo walked over to me at the end and said, "You know, everything he said sounded to me like 'Jabberwocky,' but I am sold on this unitrust idea." He subsequently signed up for the $1.3 million unitrust and transformed that day into a huge success.

And that's how we got back to Lewis Carroll.

CHAPTER FIFTY-SIX
The Craziness of the
Concert Business

This is not a tell-all book about everything wrong in the fundraising field. I leave that to the gossipers, rumor mongers and TMZ. But there are times when every professional asks himself or herself, *Am I crazy, or is the work I am engaged in crazy?* I can say, unequivocally, this is how I felt when producing benefit concerts.

Before I get into some of the craziness, allow me to delineate three criteria that I formulated, and which guided me whether to hold a benefit concert. The most influential criterion was whether the event would be financially successful. For this, I always drafted a budget in advance, showing a realistic projection of expected revenues and expenses. Every organization must decide for itself its respectable profit, the bottom line. What works for you may not work for the next nonprofit. But I would rank this as the most pressing priority.

The second criterion is assessing the public relations and marketing value of the event. As you peruse through this book, you will read about how public relations and marketing efforts complement a fundraising program. Concerts can have a widespread and lasting public relations value and branding benefit for the organization. When I produced the Jewish Hospice concerts, it was at a time when the hospice concept was still in its infancy in the greater Jewish community. Many folks didn't understand what hospice was and, generally fearful of terminal care or its stigma, veered away from this service. After several concerts, word began to spread everywhere about the beneficial outcomes on patient and family. They helped educate the public, which in turn saw a slow, but concomitant, rise in the patient census.

The final criterion is the artistic or aesthetic value of a concert and how it reflects on the perceived excellence of the institution. If folks attend and see a preeminent event, this conveys subliminal and overt messages of great import. It validates that the nonprofit is involved in programs of excellence. A cardinal rule that I followed throughout my career was always to produce or take part in programs that were nothing less than excellent. It may have cost a little more, but it was worth it. That's the model I recommended to nonprofits.

Now, on to the craziness of the concert business.

There are three primary areas of concern that I bring to the attention of the reader here. Believe me there are many other items I could list, but I rank these on top:

1) Performers
2) Venue
3) Ticket sales

Performers

Would you like the good news first? In all the years I ran major concerts for different organizations, *only three* performers ever volunteered their time. I choose not to mention who out of respect to each. They would, otherwise, be hounded until their last day for freebies, and this would be patently unfair to them.

That being said, one of them was mainly interested in self-promotion. But I never look a gift horse in the mouth, and I appreciated the fact that this well-known performer stepped up (with a choir, no less) and performed at no cost to the nonprofit.

Now for the bad news—almost every performer I recruited usually wanted what you and I may consider obscene payment for their services. Truth be told, I cannot fault them. If they are in high demand, and this is their chief means of making a living, can you blame them? It's a business, and the sooner you understand that, the sooner you can get on with your business. Nevertheless, the myth that most entertainers "donate" their services is just that, a myth. Some performers and/ or their handlers also were downright nasty when negotiating their compensation, and this didn't sit well with me. But, as they say, "the show must go on."

One more word about performers—some have other *crazy* requirements too. One internationally known entertainer stipulated at contract signing a list of food preconditions that would make Dr. Atkins cringe. It consisted of three pages with fine print requesting expensive dried fruits, a variety of exotic nuts and foods with whole grains. This performer hardly touched the food before or after that concert, and it went mostly to the local food pantry. On the other hand, I remember hiring the late comedians Alan King and Stiller and Meara. All King wanted was a gin and tonic on a barstool onstage. That's it. Stiller and Meara wanted nothing.

Venue

Choosing the right venue is crucial to your success. Here's why. As realtors like to say, "It's location, location, location." For the most part, I chose Manhattan's Lincoln Center. Let me explain why. It meant that we brought in a more elite and affluent sponsor. Manhattan and Lincoln Center denote a higher sense of exclusivity. Keep in mind that regular admission tickets don't usually decide your profit. It's the patrons and benefactors who are willing to pay for the poshness of a special reception, meeting the performers, plush seating and other privileges. That's reality.

That's the good news.

Now for the not-so-great news—placing an event in a Manhattan type of location or picking a venue like Lincoln Center means you will pay a premium for the privilege. It also means that you likely will have to contend with a unionized facility. A unionized hall always costs more. I offer this example without exaggeration. One union required four stagehands to carry a few chairs from one side of the stage to the other. One stagehand would have sufficed and been cost efficient. Look up the definition of "featherbedding." Thus, you need to account for the additional expense if you go into a unionized hall. That's reality.

Ticket Sales

There are two main aspects of this issue to consider. The first is the logistical method used to sell tickets: over the phone, online, at the ticket window or through an intermediary. Often in a classy venue, management may insist on printing the tickets (another charge, of course) and may have strange requirements such as withholding some tickets for *their* constituents, or for some other inane reason. Be prepared.

The second facet to consider is your sleep quotient. What I mean is this: You hope that you have designed a captivating program that will draw a capacity crowd. I can assure you that I spent many a sleepless night tossing and turning anxious about ticket sales, even though we always sold out. It comes with the territory. Stock up on the Ambien. That's reality.

Other Considerations

Space doesn't allow me to articulate in detail other considerations, but suffice it to say there are many, including the following:

1) Choosing a master of ceremonies
2) Conflicting events you don't know about in advance that will affect your attendance
3) Audio-visual requirements
4) Marketing and advertising strategies
5) Food for the performers, staff and crew
6) Special equipment requirements
7) Signage
8) Printing needs
9) Rehearsal options, inside and outside the hall
10) Supplemental fundraising techniques

There is so much more I could add. Much, much more craziness too.

So, when you're ready, have your people call my people.

STRATEGIC FUNDRAISING GROUP LLC

CHAPTER FIFTY-SEVEN
Endow Me

It's time to unravel the mystery of endowment funds.

Actually, it's no mystery. But many professionals may not fully understand the concept, and hence this chapter to simplify matters. It's one of the major categories of fundraising, no different than annual campaigns, capital giving or planned giving.

An endowment fund, simply put, is a fund created with the intent of endowing a program or project, often in perpetuity. The principal is not invaded, and the interest generated by the fund is used to fund the program or item. After the term of the endowment fund expires, the organization might be able to use both principal and interest as it sees fit.

As a practical matter, the board of directors sets the policy for endowment funds and determines whether these should even be established by the nonprofit. Preferably, there is a strategic fundraising blueprint in place that addresses such projects.

Here is an example. Mr. and Mrs. Jack Philanthropist start a childcare service for single mothers who need a place where their child can be cared for during the day while they work. So, they set up The Jack and Lydia Philanthropist Child Care Endowment Fund. They donate $1 million to create the fund. The service is funded via investments, dividends or profits that generate 5 percent, or $50,000, per year.

Thusly, the childcare service operates *only* using the $50,000 interest. As Mr. and Mrs. Philanthropist, or other contributors, add to the fund, which is permissible, additional interest may be generated over time, and this is the income used to finance the daily operations of the childcare service.

Another instance may be when a donor wants to be sure that the infrastructure of the institution always is properly maintained, such as a roof that needs replacement. Mr. Donor establishes the Mr. Donor Infrastructure Endowment Fund contributing a $500,000 grant to create the fund. Using the same yearly investments that generate a 5 percent rate of return described above, $25,000 may be spent annually, as needed, towards the repair and/or replacement of the roof, providing the donor approves.

There are, of course, different protocols that must be instituted so that the principal remains intact and only the interest generated is used. Likewise, these rules will control who can recommend allocations, how frequently they are made, validating reasons the money is used and related restrictions, if any. This way endowment funds aren't just distributed helter-skelter. There must be a formalized system in place to make certain that the funds are used with integrity per their established purpose. In my view, this is done best through coordination by the CEO, senior fundraising executive, philanthropists and the board of directors.

Raising the funds to establish and grow an endowment fund is something that senior executives, philanthropists and the board should plan. In one case in which I was directly involved, an anonymous donor proclaimed that all donations to the organization's endowment fund would be matched dollar for dollar. These gifts came on top of contributions to the annual dinner. Thus, donors were challenged to give to the annual gala and, at the same time, support the organization with a matched gift to the endowment fund.

Endowment funds sometimes go by other names. For example, some are called "rainy day" funds because the donor wants the money to be used for contingencies not normally covered in the operating or capital budgets. I know that accountants and financial authorities will disagree with me, but these funds also are sometimes called "sinking" funds or "depreciation" funds because the money used for major capital items are not covered by other means. For those who disagree with my characterization, you may go ahead and write your own book.

As indicated before, building an endowment fund is one of the four major pillars of fundraising along with annual giving, capital campaigns and planned giving. It behooves the nonprofit to incorporate an endowment fund giving campaign, when practical, with the others. This means that if the institution's survival relies solely on using the revenue it raises annually, but cannot afford to divert funds elsewhere, so be it. In the long term, though, an endowment fund plays an essential role for an organization that wishes to fortify its future and not just rely on annual gifts that may make up the bulk of the operating budget.

My question to the nonprofit is whether it can feasibly include an endowment fund drive as part of its ongoing campaigns. Identifying specific programs donors can consider goes a long way towards planting this idea in their minds.

Major universities are known to carry billions of dollars in their endowment coffers. But they have in place established methods for raising huge amounts of revenue. Emblazoning the slogan "Endow Me" on a t-shirt, however, won't be the way to go about it.

CHAPTER FIFTY-EIGHT
Don't Give Up!

One of my favorite times of the year always was the annual Labor Day Muscular Dystrophy telethon hosted by Jerry Lewis. Seeing the amazing lineup of stars that entertained us was quite a spectacle. But truthfully, the most emotional part of the telethon, aside from "Jerry's Kids," was the grand finale twenty-four hours later when Jerry sat on his stool, lit only by a spotlight, gripping his mic and walking off with an emotional rendering of Rodgers and Hammerstein's "You'll Never Walk Alone." That moment always brought a lump to my throat and my eyes welled up with tears. Jerry faded into the night until the following year, having raised critical funds for the charity.

The lyrics of the song inspired me and are particularly apropos to fundraisers or volunteers who get easily frustrated when struggling to raise money for their charity.

When you walk through a storm
Keep your chin up high
And don't be afraid of the dark
At the end of a storm is a golden sky
And the sweet silver song of a lark
Walk on through the wind
Walk on through the rain
Tho' your dreams
Be tossed and blown
Walk on

Walk on
With hope in your heart
And you'll never walk alone
You'll never walk alone

When I began a career in fundraising, I learned that you might strike paydirt only once in every twenty phone calls to prospective contributors. So, I set my sights on getting to call #20. Guess what? There were times when I got to call #30, #40 and beyond, but still no luck. My motto became "Don't give up!" So, Jerry's yearly swansong was an inspiration as I marched on. In today's age of advanced technology, cold calling has become more problematic unless combined with a proven list of donors to the charity. But you can't give up!

A far more effective approach in obtaining charitable gifts was setting up appointments to meet donors in their home, place of business or on neutral terrain such as a restaurant. Today, this has become more challenging for various reasons. Unless you are well connected with the philanthropist, getting a "cold" appointment is an arduous task. Here are some reasons why.

For one, you must get past the gatekeeper to secure the appointment. Receptionists, secretaries and administrative assistants are no longer as cooperative as they once were, because their bosses trained them accordingly.

Technology tells them who is calling. And after the first meeting, even leaving behind a box of chocolates for the assistant is no longer in vogue. As the wise Forrest Gump said, "Life is like a box of chocolates. You never know what you're gonna get." No appointments are guaranteed.

And donors themselves have become more sophisticated in eluding professional fundraisers. If you are in a large metropolitan area, getting into a high-rise apartment or office building is quite an undertaking. Unless you arranged in advance to meet the prospect, getting past security is no mean feat. Your personal identification is no longer enough. The donor must place you on their list of approved guests. And now some buildings have a "Deny entry" request in place for some guests. Oy vey!

In-person galas are making a slow comeback now that mass vaccinations are putting the pandemic behind us. But some older benefactors, Baby Boomers who account for the bulk of charitable contributions in the United States, are still wary of the efficacy of the vaccines. They are not so anxious to find themselves in crowds. Nonetheless, in time, with the effectiveness of the injections and with the bringing about of herd immunity, this concern may dissipate.

Thomas Edison once said, "Our greatest weakness lies in giving up. The most certain way to succeed is always to try just one more time." Life is full of challenges, and giving up might be just one step away from success.

We should, therefore, take to heart what is learned in *Ethics of our Fathers*, 2:21: "It is not incumbent on you to finish the task, but neither are you free to absolve yourself from it." We are expected to put in the maximum effort and do our best.

So as the song goes, "Keep your chin up high . . . At the end of a storm is a golden sky, And the sweet silver song of a lark." With hope in your heart, know that you will never walk alone if you keep going, even when the path is strewn with obstacles and is arduous to navigate.

These are just some thoughts that are grist for the mill. As they say, don't be farklempt and go talk amongst yourselves.

CHAPTER FIFTY-NINE
When You Need a
Fundraising Consultant

I will undoubtedly be accused of writing this as a self-serving chapter. After all, in 2012, I established a firm called Strategic Fundraising Group and through it provide consulting services to the nonprofit world with an emphasis on fundraising. Ok, I get it. Nonetheless, there are not-for-profit organizations that greatly benefit by using an objective consultant to help them raise vital funds and that is, *sincerely*, why I decided to write this essay. Really.

Why Hire a Consultant?

There are numerous reasons why a fundraising consultant can be of benefit to a nonprofit institution. First, it gives the organization experience-based expertise that it may not have on its own. Presumably, the consultant has a history of fundraising success from which to draw upon and share with the leadership of the nonprofit.

Another common-sense reason to hire a consultant is to acquire philanthropic advice and counsel that will give indispensable guidance on how to go about raising needed funds. Some folks are operations oriented, and their sole attention, understandably, is directed to running the charity, not on raising funds. Some are devoted to the cause, but shy away from asking folks to give to it even though they must have funding to exist.

Some consultants are tasked with the responsibility to develop a strategic plan that becomes the blueprint for the organization on how to go about achieving fundraising success. The experience and background of some leadership running a nonprofit, lay and professional, are primarily focused on supplying services for which it was set up. A strategic plan helps show and prioritize what is important, and indicates how the nonprofit should use its resources in raising the revenues necessary to make ends meet.

Competition also drives the need to hire a consultant to equip the organization with an "edge" in how it secures funds from foundations, donor-advised funds and other major gifts. There are about 1.6 million registered nonprofits in the United States, and there are many similar organizations whose missions overlap sometimes in the same catchment area. Having the guidance of an experienced consultant can give the institution an understanding on how to distinguish itself from its competitors. I call it the "Ma-Nishtana factor" (Hebrew from the Passover Seder where the youngest child asks, "Why is this night different from all other nights?").

Cost-efficiency is another good reason to bring in a consultant. The smaller to moderately sized nonprofits may not have the wherewithal to afford hiring a full-time fundraiser and, thereby, pay a salary and benefits commensurate with the position. A consultant is usually paid as an independent contractor and can work flexibly, full or part-time, and still achieve dramatic results.

Some volunteer and professional leadership simply do not have the knowledge base or even the gumption to ask a donor for a major gift. They may be enthusiastic about everything else, but not how to properly make the ask. They are always prepared to make personal sacrifices to help the organization, *except* for this one important duty. However, philanthropy is a key responsibility of lay leaders on top of governance and advocacy, and should not be overlooked. Often these nonprofits need help in this integral area of fundraising.

These are some compelling reasons why I believe there are instances when it pays to hire a consultant to help the nonprofit raise money.

But what should the consultant do?

What to Look for in a Consultant

If you are looking to hire philanthropic counsel, there are key elements in his/her background and job description that should be considered, including the following ten qualities:

1) Does the consultant have a history of financial success? Foremost, choosing one should be contingent on a history of raising funds successfully in the nonprofit world.
2) Does the consultant supply advice only, or will he/she be willing to solicit donors, if this is needed?
3) How knowledgeable is the consultant about traditional as well as newer methods of fundraising, including donor software and the latest technologies?
4) Can the consultant collaborate with the organization's leaders and recommend a strategic fundraising plan that will serve as a map with pathways to success?
5) Dealing with different publics such as volunteers, lay leaders, donors and other professionals requires a certain type of personality, temperament and stamina. Is the consultant's character one that will mesh with these various groups?
6) Does the consultant have a good reputation for being ethical and forthright as one of his/her qualifications?

7) Does the consultant provide you with a written agreement that has SMART (Specific, Measurable, Attainable, Relevant and Time-measured) goals in it?

8) Are the consultant's fees affordable in relation to what must be raised (cost-benefit)?

9) Does the consultant know the community with important linkages to philanthropists? Or will he/she rely on your leadership for these connections?

10) Is the consultant interested in, knowledgeable and enthusiastic about your cause?

There are, of course, other considerations such as good communication skills, excellence in follow up, experience in all major categories of fundraising or, at least, in your specialized area, familiarity with your culture and someone who can provide excellent references.

There you are. Now go out and raise a lot of money.

CHAPTER SIXTY
Respect

"I'm better than you!"

"No, I'm better than you!"

"I know more than you do!

"No, I know more than you do!"

Sounds like bickering among children. Remember this one, "Sticks and stones . . ."? You know the rest.

So, what am I referring to? With slight hyperbole, but with seriousness, I refer to the unspoken but palpable tension that exists between lay leaders and professional fundraisers—some, not all.

In *Ethics of our Fathers* there is a well-known truism about "derech eretz," which literally means the "way of the land," but totally loses in the translation. What it refers to is proper conduct, good manners or good behavior. The saying found in *Pirkei Avot* 3:17 is, "Without derech eretz there can be no Torah, and without Torah, there can be no derech eretz." In my opinion it means "respect," and the saying demonstrates the profound importance of interpersonal respect among sentient beings. For lay leadership and professionals to successfully collaborate, there needs to exist a profound mutual respect. Without it, failure becomes the only possibility.

My experience is one of every so often finding unhealthy tension between these two worlds, tension I have experienced, as well as tension I have seen others go through. Regrettably, I have observed it at Jewish federations, Jewish community centers, Jewish family service agencies and other Jewish nonprofits too.

Let me recount one story that happened to me.

It is my unambiguous feeling that, when an organization hires a seasoned professional with a record of success and the requisite due diligence was performed on the individual hired, then it's time for lay leaders to stand down and allow the professional to do his/her job. Don't confuse this with not conducting proper oversight. Of course, when it comes to governance, that is a necessary component of a board's responsibility.

No, I refer to the undesirable quality of some board members to micromanage, a major source of unhealthy tension. Some lay leaders regularly pursue this course of action, and it is only to the detriment of the organization and certainly undermines the sense of mutual respect both lay and professional entities need to be successful. My philosophy is not one shared by all lay leadership, but that's understandable because it works the other way around too.

In my view, micromanagement is disrespectful and unacceptable unless the professional grossly mismanages his/her job. It also is one short step away from bullying.

Let me cite an example.

I was hired by a highly respectable nonprofit that knew of my fundraising abilities and acumen. They had gone through a lengthy process of recruitment and were fortunate to hire me (if I conceitedly say so myself). Micromanagement and looking over the professional's shoulder, however, were immediate telltale signs why this organization could not consistently retain its senior executives.

One Passover, my wife and I flew to Florida to celebrate the holiday in Boynton Beach. It is important to keep in mind that there are certain times of the year when most Jewish philanthropists arrange to leave home and go elsewhere for the holiday. Trying to solicit donors in person at that time of year is truly an effort in futility. For example, the last two weeks of August also are a traditional time when fundraisers usually face a vast fundraising wasteland because most philanthropists disappear into the netherworld, a vacuum called vacation.

And so, one Passover, when normally I am away, I get a call from the chairman of the board. I had the lay leader on loudspeaker when he thundered at me: "How dare you leave now! How can you do this to the (name of the organization)! You had no right to go away. What chutzpah . . ." and on and on and on. My wife had just entered the room and was horrified by the tone, language and attitude of this leader. Mind you that the organization was informed that I am always away for the major holidays.

There is a code of conduct, derech eretz, that should always exist between the lay leader and the professional. It's important for peaceful coexistence. This was one time when it was egregiously violated. And I will never forget it.

While that was an intimidating experience, I was resolved not to let it slide. My advice to veteran professionals, nay all professionals, is to engender an atmosphere of mutual respect. When something like this happens, the professional needs to artfully "push back," preferably when it occurs, but always, even if only eventually. The communication should be done assertively but not aggressively, appropriately but not disrespectfully. Language and tone should be moderate, but to the point. Otherwise, the professional will always be pushed around, and that doesn't make for a healthy work environment.

It is said, "Derech eretz kadma l'Torah." Respect even precedes the study of Torah. No one is immune to this mandate, neither the lay leader nor the professional.

And remember this: "...and names will never hurt me."

CHAPTER SIXTY-ONE
Planting the Seeds

I was just putting the finishing touches on my book when the phone rang. It was my grandson Donny. A call from a grandchild usually means supporting a school fundraising project. That's fine; I welcome it. Sure enough . . .

> Donny: "Hi Sabba (Hebrew for "grandfather"). How are you?"
> Me: "I'm good. What's up?"
> Donny: "I was wondering if you could help me with a school project."
> Me: "Sure. What can I do for you?"
> Donny: "My class is raising money for the school."
> Me: (*Ok. Here it comes*).
> Donny: "Can you post my school's project on your social media?"

Wow! This wasn't any ordinary ask. What Donny was asking was whether I could be an influencer for his school's matching gift campaign. Smart. He wasn't asking me outright for a donation (which he presumably knew I was going to make anyway). He was beyond that. What he really was asking for was whether I would be willing to spread the word far and wide about his school's matching gift campaign, thereby influencing others to give. He wanted me to use my social media as a conduit to spread the word. Donny's high school had only twenty-four hours in which to raise $100,000, and the way to cast a larger net and catch more fish was to contact me, among others, to persuade a larger group of donors, our social media contacts, to give.

The way this and similar campaigns work is simply as follows. The nonprofit has a limited amount of time to reach its preset financial goal (in this case $100,000). The amount of time is usually between twenty-four to thirty-six hours during which a full court press is made to reach out to donors via phone calls, online approaches and even through personal visits, which, if they result in gifts, are recorded live online.

To set the stage, the nonprofit must have three critical audiences with which it interacts: (1) influencers, (2) matchers and (3) donors. The influencers encompass a larger number of individuals that can influence others to participate in the campaign. The matchers, often major philanthropists, actually commit to sizable sums of money that are used to match oftentimes dollar for dollar towards what donors contribute. And, of course, there are the regular donors who contribute during this exciting albeit time-limited campaign. And everyone can monitor the dynamic progress online as the mercury rises during the heat of this dynamic campaign.

That's how it works.

But truth be told, this matching gift campaign is not the purpose of my essay. What Donny's call really triggered was a far more important aspect of fundraising—the involvement of young leadership. They are the future, and it is this topic that actually deserves our special attention.

Allow me to digress and introduce the name Arnold van Gennep, a folklorist and ethnographer of French-German-Dutch extraction. He was perhaps best known for studying rites of passage in various cultures. Van Gennep developed a great insight called "liminality," which has perfect applicability here. Dictionary.com defines liminality as a state of transition between one stage and the next, especially between major stages in one's life or during a rite of passage. Thus, it is very apropos to our discussion.

An example of a liminal space might be a stairwell that by itself is empty, but serves as a necessary passageway from one floor to the next. Another example is an airport lobby, which serves as a way to get from one airport terminal to another. By themselves, liminal spaces are just conduits to another location, but they are critical to get from one point to the next.

I view young leadership as the living and breathing liminal space between the nonprofit's present and its future potential. As a rule, volunteers are the lifeblood of any organization. Young leadership falls into this category, and for a nonprofit to blossom, it cannot just rely on the Baby Boomers who will eventually fade away in time. The Millennials that will follow will have their own challenges (discussed in the chapter "The Great Divide: Millennials vs. Baby Boomers"). The next generation up at bat is the high schooler who is going through his/her own rites of passage—in between the liminal state of transition to young leadership—and who will become critical to the essential growth of the nonprofit.

The time to plant fertile seeds and have them take root is now. Poet and novelist Robert Louis Stevenson is quoted as saying, "Don't judge each day by the harvest you reap but by the seeds you plant." Soon, these future leaders will seek out career routes that may very well intersect with the nonprofits. Nurturing this group through fundraisers like matching gift campaigns is exactly the type of encouragement they need while their fertile minds are educated in the ways of charitable giving.

By the way, when Donny's campaign ended, he told me with great pride and a sense of personal accomplishment that his class had raised

$21,000 towards their campaign. If we can fertilize that enthusiasm, nonprofits will surely prosper.

Way to go, Donny!

CHAPTER SIXTY-TWO
The Transition Plan

You have given proper notice to your current employer, and now it's time to look forward to the next stepping stone in your career. Or, perhaps, you are about to enter retirement. Another possibility is that you decided to launch a new business opportunity, which is the reason you are leaving. Or, maybe, you just needed to take time off. Of course, it's also possible that you were let go. There are many reasons why folks exit their employment.

I am often asked, "What are your obligations to the employer from whom you are taking leave?" Is it ok to just become a "lame duck," put your career on cruise control and then be done with it? My short answer, especially if you are an ethical fundraiser, is a resounding, "No!" In my considered opinion, you have a moral and professional responsibility to make your exit a smooth, painless and even a righteous one.

Remember, too, that you never want to "burn your bridges" behind you and besmirch your good name. Tarnishing your reputation will do you no good. Benjamin Franklin once said, "Glass, china and reputation are easily cracked, and never well mended." So, how honorably you handle your employment termination may indeed herald your career or retirement life forwards. It is like starting the last chapter in a book; you still look for a happy ending.

The Association of Fundraising Professionals adopted a code of ethical principles and standards. Oddly, there are no canons it specifically adopted to deal with issues of when an employee leaves employment. However, it is understood that the existing standards apply to development executives who are yet working for their employer. It would follow that, even after service to the nonprofit, certain principles are still in play. These would include the following standards:

> Practice their profession with integrity, honesty, truthfulness and adherence to the absolute obligation to safeguard the public trust . . . demonstrate concern for the interests and well-being of individuals affected by their actions . . . Bring credit to the fundraising profession by their public demeanor.

However, it is my contention that professionals have a moral obligation to leave behind a transition plan that will not only enhance their reputation, but also pave the way to success by a successor (notice how the word "success" is embedded in the word "successor"). Leaving with grace is just as crucial as the promise you held out when you joined the organization. Who knows? You may be fortunate enough to recruit your replacement.

The format of the transition plan will depend on the importance of your job, as well as the size of your nonprofit and the scope of your responsibilities and job description. In this regard, the plan might be as simple as just preparing a checklist of tasks and previous assignments, ranging all the way to a comprehensive plan describing many details.

Here are some of the key elements in the transition plan you should consider including when leaving your employer:

1) Schedule an exit interview: Meet with your supervisor and/ or lay leadership before leaving. This is a good opportunity to review highlights of your written transition plan. It also is an opportunity to enhance your reputation by saying thank you and comporting yourself humbly. It's always a smart idea

to leave a good taste in everyone's mouth by keeping it nice and polite.

2) Update your portfolio: Every fundraiser supports a list of donors during their tenure. These are philanthropists for whom they are responsible, and the plan should include important facts such as contact information, birthdays and anniversaries, friendships/relationships and special circumstances to be aware of such as a description of the donor's idiosyncrasies.

3) Offer your point of view and suggestions: The transition plan is an opportunity to respectfully share ideas about your donors and prospects. You have accumulated knowledge that shouldn't go to waste. What a wonderful chance to show your erudition about the subject matter with which you are most familiar, such as potential honorees and sponsors. You may be leaving, but depart as a champion for your former cause. Your helpful ideas may also mend some broken fences that may bode well for you in your next position.

4) Address the four major categories of giving: Unless you were not responsible for them, the transition plan should incorporate your plans, where relevant, for the annual campaign, capital campaign, planned giving and endowment fund giving. When possible, include the status of major gifts, special events, legacies and bequests, foundation grants, grassroots campaigns and all other forms of giving in which you were personally involved such as direct mail, appeals and special development strategies.

So, do you need to create transition plan when you resign from a job? No, but you want to because it's the right thing to do.

INTRODUCTION TO THE SPECIAL COVID-19 PANDEMIC SECTION

Never in modern history has a pandemic like COVID-19 befallen us. Yes, the Spanish Flu hit the US shores in 1918, and it was a monster contagion. Like this COVID-19 pandemic and its variants, it also came in multiple waves, and it is estimated that, as a result, anywhere between 20 million to 50 million persons died worldwide, possibly more. It also is estimated that 675,000 Americans died. While some of the numbers are in question, suffice to say, it was a catastrophic pandemic much as the coronavirus has been in the modern era.

The COVID-19 pandemic was first identified in December 2019 in Wuhan, China. Despite having spread to two countries in its infancy, most public health authorities did not initially declare it to be a public health emergency. When it arrived in the United States in January 2020, no one was prepared to predict the magnitude of this disease here and throughout the world. That changed rapidly, and today multiple millions have died around the globe and scores and scores of millions more were infected.

I wrote a number of newspaper columns that were published during the COVID-19 pandemic, and there are lessons to be gleaned from these in the event we are ever revisited by another pandemic and its variants. And it is likely we will. Hopefully not, but in case similar circumstances occur again, it is worth considering whether there are fundraising commonalities, although with probable variations.

Ironically, 2020 saw one of the most successful fundraising years in the United states ever.

This section is dedicated to all those who perished during this unprecedented medical event in modern history, as well as to those who were deeply affected by this disease, either having caught the virus themselves and/or those who lost family and friends to this highly contagious disease.

May we and our descendants never suffer through such a horrifying calamity again.

CHAPTER SIXTY-THREE
Will the COVID-19 Pandemic
Affect Fundraising?

Will the COVID-19 pandemic affect fundraising?

Anyone who can answer this question deserves the Fortune Teller of the Century award. No one can say with certainty how this story will end, but we can conjecture on the basis of earlier calamities.

Let's state the obvious. We never experienced anything like the COVID-19 pandemic in our lifetimes. Ever. And, God willing, we should never again face such a catastrophic event. But we might glean trend patterns from history.

There are three relatively recent financial disasters from which to draw inferences: (1) the 1987 financial crash, (2) 9/11/2001 and (3) the 2008 Great Recession and housing collapse. Each of these events triggered great national financial devastation. The difference now, however, is this. Those events did not wreak the same massive havoc this COVID-19 pandemic is inflicting on the economy.

The 1987 Financial Crash

October 19, 1987, also known as "Black Monday," saw the Dow Jones Industrial Average plunge by 22.6 percent causing a sudden and dramatic global stock market decline. The cause was not attributable to some financial crisis or a growing recession. Instead, markets tumbled largely because of massive computer program, or digital, trading that manipulated vast numbers of stocks and financial portfolios. We also suffered through a chain reaction of financial distress factors such as the trading of risky securities, a declining dollar and hard-to-understand algorithms egged on by a 24/7 media hysteria.

The economy eventually stabilized, and stocks recovered. The 1987 financial crisis established the *essential* circuit breakers that pause trading when stocks dive to scary depths marked by percentage markers. There also were other structural flaws in the market that aggravated losses. However, this is not the forum to discuss these, but is an opportunity to see how fundraising fared during that era of financial turmoil.

Unlike the 1929 Depression that took decades from which to bounce back, the 1987 crash rebounded within two years and topped previous market levels. The Federal Reserve was a calming influence that added liquidity to the economy. New regulatory reforms helped steady markets. Fundraising made a comeback commensurate with the economic rebound. It took time, but recovery occurred because of renewed confidence in the monetary system.

9/11/2001

9/11 was a pivotal moment in history, and it caused Wall Street to shut down for an unnerving six-day period rocking financial markets everywhere.

Investopedia recounts how bad the markets reacted. "On the first day of NYSE trading after 9/11, the market fell 684 points, a 7.1% decline, setting a record at the time for the biggest loss in exchange history for one trading day"—this was since eclipsed by the market reaction during the global COVID-19 pandemic —"At the close of trading that Friday, ending a week that saw the biggest losses in NYSE history, the Dow Jones was down almost 1,370 points, representing a loss of over 14%. The S&P index lost 11.6%. An estimated $1.4 trillion in value was lost in those five days of trading."

Yet, the *NonProfit Times* reported that "despite the challenges of September 11 and a slowing economy, nearly 60 percent of charities raised more money in 2001 than in 2000." A survey in the *NonProfit Times* also showed that "an additional 10 percent of charities raised the same amount of money in 2001 as in 2000, and slightly more than 15 percent of respondents raised at least 30 percent more funds."

Not more than a month passed before the Dow Jones, Nasdaq and S&P regained their pre-9/11 price levels. So, what prompted donors to be generous at a time when financial markets were shaken?

Here are some factors to consider: A united country was motivated to pull itself up by the bootstraps, and show terrorists and the entire world that America wouldn't capitulate to terror. Also, many believe that philanthropy always rallies during times of crisis and a new normal sets in.

2008 Recession

The Great Recession of 2008 was linked to the subprime mortgage crisis. The stock market rocketed to greater heights after a period of recuperation following the Great Recession. However, in a blog post for CCS by author Tyler Mark, the executive director of CCS Fundraising, wrote,

> The U.S. economy was in the depths of the most devastating economic downturn since the Great Depression. The impact was substantial and widespread when 8.8 million people lost their jobs, GDP fell more than 4%, and home prices deteriorated by 30%. At the same time, Americans collectively gave less to charities than they had since the 1990s.

Mark continued, "However, despite the resiliency of Americans during tough economic times, the Great Recession's deep and widespread impact left many people giving less. Giving decreased by 3.7% in 2008 and then 8.3% in 2009. Much of this drop can be attributed to declines in giving by the wealthiest Americans."

Nevertheless, in time, the economy strengthened and rallied. It took time. But fundraising also bounced back because the American people recognized the plight of the needy and less fortunate and responded accordingly.

COVID-19 Pandemic

Here is what we knew at the time of this writing.

The COVID-19 pandemic brought the US economy to a virtual halt with some exceptions. There were grave concerns that many small businesses, the bedrock of America's commerce, went bankrupt or out of business. US Treasury Secretary Mnuchin, part of the Trump administration, suggested that unemployment could rocket to 20 percent, which many considered to be a conservative estimate. Stocks tumbled to the extent of wiping out all the gains made in the last three years prior to the pandemic. Major industries such as the auto industry came to a standstill, and on a war footing, auto plants converted their factories into ventilator production. The health-care industry was expected to be overwhelmed and unable to handle all the cases coming its way. And the list of bad news piled on as the COVID-19 disaster rippled throughout the economy.

So, what can we learn from earlier financial debacles? We can only surmise how this story may end.

If the panacea provided by the original $2 trillion stimulus works in tandem with effective treatment protocols and the vaccines work, there is no reason to believe fundraising won't rebound as in previous disasters.

Let's not consider the alternative.

NOTE: The vaccines discovered were effective, and as businesses reopened and lockdowns were lifted, fundraising in the United States achieved new highs. At the time of publication, however, concerns arose regarding the variants and rising COVID-19 cases in the United States, although deaths and hospitalizations plummeted. It seemed, however, that we had turned the corner on this disease.

STRATEGIC
FUNDRAISING
GROUP LLC

CHAPTER SIXTY-FOUR
Would You Like to Attend
my Virtual Parlor Meeting?

No one could have predicted on January 1, 2020, what a topsy-turvy year it would be with the COVID-19 pandemic. The most skilled crystal ball gazer would have been ridiculed. We were in the throes of a pandemic never envisioned in our lifetime, economic turmoil unlike anything experienced since 1929 and societal upheavals where conventional values and mores were ripped asunder and fell like toppling statues (literally).

The *Boston Business Journal* reported before mid-year that Massachusetts nonprofits lost $8.6 billion during the COVID-19 pandemic. Imagine Canada estimated the financial impact on registered charities in Canada to be between $9.5 and $15.7 billion. Seismic losses in the billions were also experienced in the United States.

In view of this, nonprofit organizations everywhere were collectively scratching their heads trying to figure out what to do with their fundraising plans. Two fail-safe methods to raise large funds—major gift solicitations and major events—took big hits for obvious reasons.

Major gift giving still occurred, but had to overcome many hurdles. Social distancing and wearing a mask make it increasingly difficult to make appointments with major donors. Inevitably, philanthropists, older

Baby Boomers who were the most susceptible to transmission, were reluctant to waive self-sheltering to meet one-on-one with fundraisers.

Attending a major event, such as a gala, came to a screeching halt. These became excruciatingly difficult considering people were not rushing out to get infected by someone carrying the disease. Who wanted to take a chance and be the recipient of a fatal virus? How was that smorgasbord coming along? It wasn't.

What were nonprofits doing?

A quick survey showed that nonprofits were banking on their good reputations to virtually spirit their way through the COVID-19 pandemic and raise money. Here is what some did.

Eli Beer, founder of United Hatzalah in Israel, came down with the virus. It was an amazing story of someone who fought for his life and recovered. United Hatzalah initially held a virtual event, "Saving Lives Sunday," featuring stars such as Jay Leno, Rona-Lee Shimon and Lior Suchard in a salute to first responders. In addition, Eli constantly shared his and other heroic stories on social media to keep their names in the public square. Unending messages from Beer and luminaries such as then US ambassador to Israel, David Friedman, kept appearing with the vigor of the Energizer Bunny.

One Israel Fund is dedicated to supporting the welfare and safety of men, women and children of Judea, Samaria, the Jordan Valley and the communities of Gaza evacuees. It shared videos of the important work it does through regular e-blasts. They also created a virtual tour series, and ran educational webinars to initiate the uninitiated. An online lottery was held, always a popular attraction, especially with folks sheltered away. Arranging fascinating interviews with prestigious members of Israel's military was another way to show fulfillment of its mission.

Here was a novel approach. Ever attend a virtual golf, tennis and card outing? After twenty-six years and having postponed the real thing, the Jewish Home Foundation of North Jersey held a Zoom event. It featured sports figures and cameo appearances by guest celebrities, all on Zoom. This event garnered upwards of $4 million in net revenue over the years. But this was the first time it wasn't held in person. It counted on its great reputation and sponsors to carry the day.

Sharsheret raises funds to combat breast and ovarian cancer, and held a tri-state virtual benefit honoring various awardees. It relied on its sterling reputation and the beneficence of generous patrons to achieve fundraising goals. Letters, advertising, word of mouth and social media were instrumental in mass publicizing this virtual event. This was the new approach in the COVID-19 era.

A standard fundraising activity is the parlor meeting. I always joked about inviting people to a parlor meeting. In my mind, inviting folks to a parlor meeting was the sure kiss of death for attendance. Why would you want to attend a gathering where the purpose is clear? Times changed, and donors were seeking freshness. So, this revamped method on Zoom, or some other virtual means, became the new normal.

A day will come when we will resume full traditional fundraising. One thing for sure, successful nonprofits must stay in regular touch with donors. Is your nonprofit virtually there?

NOTE: The vaccines discovered were effective, and as businesses reopened and lockdowns were lifted, fundraising in the United States achieved new highs. At the time of publication, however, concerns arose regarding the variants and rising COVID-19 cases in the United States, although deaths and hospitalizations plummeted. It seemed, however, that we had turned the corner on this disease.

CHAPTER SIXTY-FIVE
Adjusting with the Times

About twenty years ago, I underwent shoulder surgery. As everyone is prone to do, I asked around, "Where can I find the *best* shoulder surgeon?" I mean the very *best* shoulder surgeon. After ample research, I found the surgeon who virtually wrote the textbook on shoulder surgery. After getting second opinion(s), I used this surgeon.

He informed me that during the surgery I would be half-awake because he needed *my help* and flexibility in moving my upper torso. In fact, he told me, I would be awake for most of the procedure. Well, I wasn't crazy about that idea, but I thought, *He's the expert; he must know.* So, I underwent the surgery, and even recall sitting up and being maneuvered around to help him get through *my* procedure. It was disconcerting, to say the least.

As circumstances would have it, a few years back, my wife also needed shoulder surgery. We did our due diligence, again, and found a different surgeon, one local to where we lived in New Jersey. He also had an excellent reputation. But, to be safe, we visited my surgeon for a second opinion, and he was most helpful. I reminisced with him how he kept me half-awake during my surgery to manipulate my upper body. He turned to me, laughed and exclaimed in a booming voice, "Oh no! I don't do that anymore. I had to adjust with the times." *What?*

Fundraising was in much the same quandary. It needed to adjust with the times. With COVID-19 affecting major fundraising events as never before, nonprofits' creative flexibility was stretched to the limits. So, what did this adjustment look like? What trended?

Ironically, a large part of fundraising successes was attributable to the COVID-19 pandemic. And creative nonprofits learned to adjust with the times. A story in the Sun Sentinel's *Florida Jewish Journal* well into the COVID-19 pandemic showed that "Jewish philanthropists have increased their giving during (the) COVID-19 pandemic." In some instances, Jewish donors also were more flexible in their grant giving because they were keenly aware of immediate social service needs due to job layoffs, housing hardships, food assistance needs and growing mental health problems. As such, philanthropists loosened up previous giving restrictions because of urgent and existential conditions. In fact, Jewish foundations and Jewish federations donated on top of existing grants when nonprofits could show that the funds would be used to ameliorate the lives of folks unemployed by the COVID-19 pandemic, or those facing emergency circumstances.

Born out of the birth pangs of COVID-19 were new and robust charitable giving opportunities where government was unable or unwilling to help. A private entrepreneur, Dave Portnoy, who founded the popular online digital media company Barstool Sports, decided he needed to do something. He raised more than $35 million to help small businesses adversely impacted by the COVID-19 pandemic. The pervasive nature of this virus causing massive business lockdowns in the country brought this charity into being. Dave Portnoy adjusted with the times.

You will recall, before COVID-19, we often saw pictures of Asians wearing face masks here and overseas. Then along came the CDC guideline, and suddenly *everyone* was wearing masks. President Biden, upon assuming office, also indicated that he wanted all Americans to wear masks during the first hundred days of his presidency to help reduce the number of infections, especially among the non-vaccinated. Clearly, all of us adjusted with the times, and wearing a mask, even as we approached bank tellers (once unheard of), has become routine now and into the foreseeable future.

Nonprofits adjusted to virtual fundraisers, albeit some outdoor-oriented events where masks and social distancing were possible made a slow but steady comeback. Online games of chance, matching gift campaigns, virtual galas or concerts, social media fundraising and Zoom parlor meetings were everywhere. Direct mail solicitations were another sure way to reach an audience, while engaging major donors on the phone or in person were again making an impact. As the editor of the *Florida Jewish Journal* editorialized at the time, "Many who never gave of themselves before are volunteering and contributing to society for the first time in their lives." *Tikkun Olam* adjusted with the times.

Without appearing crass or mercenary, it seems that *most donors were giving more money to help those most in need because of the COVID-19 pandemic.* So, I ask your nonprofit: did it adjust with the times?

NOTE: The vaccines discovered were effective, and as businesses reopened and lockdowns were lifted, fundraising in the United States achieved new highs. At the time of publication, however, concerns arose regarding the variants and rising COVID-19 cases in the United States, although deaths and hospitalizations plummeted. It seemed, however, that we had turned the corner on this disease.

STRATEGIC FUNDRAISING GROUP LLC

CHAPTER SIXTY-SIX
After the COVID-19 Pandemic, Then What?

One morning we woke up and heard the good news: a vaccine was discovered for the coronavirus, and plentiful doses were being distributed throughout the United States. You signed up, got vaccinated and, with bounteous gratitude in your heart, shook the hand of the person administering the vaccine. You might even have given that individual a hug. The end. And everyone lived happily ever after.

Not quite.

If you were a nonprofit and needed to raise funds for your organization, it wasn't business as usual. I have noted in other essays that a day will come when we will resume normal fundraising activities such as regularly meeting one-on-one with major donors and holding large galas or special events involving masses of people. However, it still won't be easy.

Here's why.

There are a group of donors who cling to doubts about the efficacy of the vaccine, regardless of what the medical experts say. We are chastened by this COVID-19 pandemic, and rightfully, our guards are up having heard conflicting news about what works and what doesn't. Baby Boomers are acutely aware that 80 percent or more of fatalities were sixty-five years of age or older and, according to news reports, it was estimated that the average age of these folks was seventy-seven. So, there are sobered groups leery of the vaccine's effectiveness. They also are legitimately concerned about the COVID-19 pandemic elsewhere in the world and how it will affect us. There is real concern about the movement of international variants and mutations. Of course, there are also the anti-vaxxers who are ringing alarm bells.

Other factors enter the picture, as well. These are divided into the following categories: (1) the state of the economy, (2) the state of peace and tranquility in cities where crime, looting and violence are out of control and (3) the state of politics dictated by political elections in the United States.

The verdict is out on the state of the economy. While the stock market has rebounded, it is but only one indicator of many to watch. GDP, Federal Reserve actions, corporate earnings, housing, inflation and hyper-inflation, unemployment figures, jobless claims, interest rates, increased government regulations and the condition of US debt compounded by trillions of stimulus dollar packages will factor in. Many are concerned that Congress is digging us into a deeper hole by printing more paper. As of this writing, and for the near future, the numbers are disturbing, and to a degree, we will not return in my opinion to optimal economic conditions as before the COVID-19 pandemic took hold.

Thousands of businesses went out of business, and will not be back or are diminished. Leading the pack are restaurants and commercial retailers that didn't survive the impact of business losses. In some cases, online companies such as Amazon, eBay, Overstock.com and others were gobbling up remaining business opportunities.

New ways of doing business will affect the future economy. Automation is spreading and relieving blue collar workers from tasks humans once held. News reports showed robots in a hair salon styling customers' hair, including washing, coloring and cutting. Self-checkouts in stores like Target, Home Depot and grocery chains enjoy the benefit of side-stepping long lines in regular checkout aisles. We also know that more automated tasks are being introduced in the automotive industry, and artificial intelligence will likely replace bookkeepers in the financial world, proofreaders in the publishing world, automated benefits systems in the HR world and the list grows.

Our country is shaking with seismic protests, lawlessness and anarchy that are decimating cities. Ongoing increases in homicides, unabated looting, arson and the formation of unsafe business districts where people are attacked and stores vandalized are sounding alarm bells. Anti-Semitic incidents, racial divisiveness and ethnic hatred have also reared their ugly heads. If these trends continue, they will instill unquelled fear in the hearts of philanthropists who are genuinely worried what these actions are doing to the country.

As statues come tumbling down and history is erased and revised, donors will not be in a mood to contribute but, instead, will hold on to savings and investments in case they need the money. This is true no matter how wealthy they are—just another psychological impediment that nonprofits need to overcome.

The 2020 elections also played into supporter concerns. This is the most progressive White House that has attached itself to the radical left. The Senate and the House are in Democrat control. Plus, there has been a shift away from the pro-business philosophy of the Trump administration. Onerous regulations are being issued, and there is a concerted effort to significantly raise taxes. Spending and the national debt may soon reach unsustainable heights as left-leaning causes such as climate change, energy cutbacks in fracking, coal and oil occur with deference to the Green New Deal, and priority is given to illegal immigrants in areas, including health care, welfare benefits and jobs. And this is the short list.

So, how will nonprofits fare after the COVID-19 pandemic? We are being injected with a new dose of reality.

NOTE: The vaccines discovered were effective, and as businesses reopened and lockdowns were lifted, fundraising in the United States achieved new highs. At the time of publication, however, concerns arose regarding the variants and rising COVID-19 cases in the United States, although deaths and hospitalizations plummeted. It seemed, however, that we had turned the corner on this disease.

CHAPTER SIXTY-SEVEN
Survival of the Fittest

Many years ago, I spoke at a conference about how nonprofit Jewish long-term care facilities might not survive unless they changed the way they did business. I suggested that areas they needed to address included fundraising effectiveness, reimbursement formulas and the need to run pristine facilities—all clean, innovative and reputable. Diverse Jewish nonprofit organizations faced similar challenges as they confronted the COVID-19 pandemic.

My recent essays tackled whether and how the COVID-19 pandemic would affect fundraising. Comparisons with previous national financial catastrophes led me to the conclusion that the United States would eventually rebound. How did Jewish nonprofits fare in the short term? The answer is obvious: many suffered from diminished fundraising, staff were furloughed and some programs closed. Why?

It goes back to my hypothesis: if there are strong fundraising and funding mechanisms in place because the nonprofits' mission resonates, and the organization is transparent and demonstrates that its good name is deserved, it would be among the fittest that survive this unprecedented financial crash.

Next, let's understand the state of the economy during COVID-19. We were hit by an economic blitzkrieg unlike anything since the Great Depression. Tens of millions were unemployed. The stock market initially lost trillions of dollars, and was the cause for pension plans and 401(k)s plunging in value, businesses closed, many to never open again or go into bankruptcy, and GDP forecasts were ghastly. Congress continued to print paper for stimulus and relief programs, but these will only bury this country in greater debt. It is a hideous situation.

The economy eventually bounced back, at least in the short term. The alternative could have been more catastrophic, so let's not walk down that path. Consequently, understanding what we mean by "Survival of the Fittest" and who got through the COVID-19 pandemic financial disaster is an imperative. Here are some key components nonprofits needed to have in place to make it through that mess.

The fundraising resiliency of nonprofits always depends on several factors. Foremost is this principle. Half of the people in this country give for one reason and one reason alone—someone asked them. If you don't ask, you won't receive.

Other cogs in the wheel are a strong online and social media presence. Have you noticed how your email inbox was besieged with e-blasts with links that took you to nonprofit websites? Facebook, Instagram and Twitter also were flooded with sponsored ads. Just know this: no presence, fewer donations. A strong direct mail program also helps.

What nonprofits must understand is why people give. Here are the most popular reasons: people rally in times of crisis to nonprofits, religious tithing (*Ma'aser* in Hebrew), some folks give to a cause like the American Cancer Society because someone they know was touched by cancer and it's a psychological rationale for self-preservation from that disease, guilt, tax benefits, a moral obligation to give, donor recognition, peer pressure and making a difference. Nonprofits must know which buttons to push to generate donations for their organizations (see chapter called "Why Do People Give?").

Those who have the resources, especially the big ones like The International Fellowship of Christians and Jews, Wounded Warriors Project, Shriners Hospital, St. Jude's Hospital, inundate the airwaves with ads because they have the financial means to do so, and while some may have seen a temporary philanthropic decline, they are strong enough to endure and power through.

One organization, Global Citizen, whose mission is to fight global poverty, raised billions of dollars through a very powerful technique. It mobilized leading celebrities to support their annual music festival. Lady Gaga, Elton John, Jennifer Hudson, Queen, Coldplay, Usher, Adam Lambert and many others brought in millions and millions of dollars to an already strong base of support. It also assembled prime ministers of countries like Canada, England, Norway, New Zealand and India among others to promote the cause. They have many other options because of their stronghold on celebrities.

Institutions of higher learning such as Harvard University, Yale, Princeton and the like have billions and billions in their endowment funds, and were least concerned about getting through the COVID-19 pandemic financial crisis. Were they worried? Of course, everyone was worried. But they knew they had the resources to survive.

Here's the bad news. It's the little guys, such as small Jewish nonprofits, which were hurt. Regrettably, those without a solid base of support, no ongoing online or social media presence, start-ups and those with little or no reserve funds faced the greatest challenge.

Charles Darwin coined the term "Survival of the Fittest," his signature phrase for evolutionary theory. Where was your nonprofit on the COVID-19 pandemic ladder?

NOTE: The vaccines discovered were effective, and as businesses reopened and lockdowns were lifted, fundraising in the United States achieved new highs. At the time of publication, however, concerns arose regarding the variants and rising COVID-19 cases in the United States, although deaths plummeted. It seemed, however, that we had turned the corner on this disease.

SIGNATURE
FUNDRAISING
GROUP LLC

EPILOGUE

And they all lived happily ever after. The end.

Isn't that how books and stories are supposed to finish? Right?

Nah! Only in fairy tales.

In the real world, not every ending in the fundraising world ends happily. Events go awry. Read chapters entitled "When Things Go Wrong, Parts I and II," and read the lessons gleaned from the special pandemic section in this book. Many a development executive can share with you the agony of defeat, having put in an endless amount of time and resources but not gotten the ROI afterwards. Sometimes it just ain't worth it.

Or as Tevye would say, "on the other hand," it's not always the short-term profit you make on your fundraising activity that matters. In the long run, sometimes, it is the formidable public relations impact that helps your development program. Sometimes it's the impressive marketing impact that makes a huge difference. Remember that robust PR and marketing programs can complement and soar your fundraising activities to grander heights (read the chapter called "Is Fundraising a Solo Act?").

For now, my sincere hope is that I have shared with you fundraising ideas that will help you succeed in your noble work.

The end. Really.

All the best,

Norm

AUTHOR'S BACKGROUND

NORMAN B. GILDIN is an experienced fundraiser guided by principles of strategic planning that have been the hallmarks of his success. His background encompasses the four major types of fundraising: annual campaigns, building fund/capital campaigns, planned giving and endowment fund giving.

Mr. Gildin believes in a well-organized, methodical approach to development. He offers a sophisticated approach to fundraising with emphasis on the strategic planning required for this task. During his career, Gildin was results oriented, and that meant getting the job done.

At Migdal Ohr, an Israeli-based organization for poor and disadvantaged children and families in Israel, he shepherded the American Office to $16.6 million raised while serving as its executive vice president.

During his tenure at OHEL Children's Home and Family Services, his leadership resulted in more than $30 million raised towards the annual campaign, and between $9-to $10 million towards the capital campaign.

In his eighteen-year tenure at Metropolitan Jewish Geriatric Foundation, Norman's leadership approach raised more than $30 million in annual and capital funds, primarily through private sector fundraising.

Norman handled the fundraising activities of the Women's Auxiliary at the Jewish Home for the Elderly of Fairfield, Connecticut, where there were one thousand members when he started and more than four thousand members at the end of his term. Early in his career, he annually raised hundreds of thousands of dollars for special events and activities at the Jewish Home.

He spearheaded multiple successful fundraising campaigns and developed strategic plans and case statements to raise essential funds.

He has strong public relations and marketing experience, and is a proven leader in the use of social media including Facebook, Twitter, LinkedIn, Tumblr, Reddit and Instagram.

Gildin is formerly a licensed nursing home administrator in New York and New Jersey. He also has lectured, published and served as a volunteer/consultant for various not-for-profit organizations. Gildin is currently a regular columnist for the Sun-Sentinel's *South Florida Jewish Journal, Gateway Gazette* and *The Jewish Link of New Jersey.*

Norman graduated magna cum laude from Yeshiva University in New York. He later obtained his master's degree in health-care administration from the George Washington University, School of Government and Business Administration, Washington, D. C.

Mr. Gildin lives with his wife Barbara in Boynton Beach, Florida, and previously lived in Teaneck, New Jersey, Bridgeport, Connecticut and Silver Spring, Maryland. They are the proud parents of five children and grandparents to sixteen grandchildren.

ABOUT STRATEGIC FUNDRAISING GROUP LLC

We live in financially challenging times when expectations are high to achieve successful fundraising results. But sometimes a development operation does not have the resources necessary to get the job done. Manpower assets may be limited, or the workload is so overwhelming that added support is essential. The work required may also extend beyond the ability of an in-house operation.

In 2012, Gildin founded a company called Strategic Fundraising Group LLC that has supplied development consultations to not-for-profit organizations. In his role as president, he has delivered quality services from small to large development operations. Depending on the nature of the service requested, Gildin has provided help in many areas including the following:

- Board, staff and volunteer training
- Special event planning
- Marketing and public relations
- Donor recognition programs
- Donor research and solicitations
- Sponsorship opportunities
- Strategic planning
- Development of case statements
- Brochure development and fulfillment
- Young leadership, auxiliary and constituency memberships
- Goal setting and achievement

- Planned giving
- Capital and endowment fund campaigns

Learn from My Experiences puts many fundamentals on the table for the nonprofit seeking knowledge and credible information on how to fundraise in their quest to achieve financial success.